THUS
SPOKE
CHANAKYA

THUS SPOKE CHANAKYA

Ancient Wisdom for Daily Inspiration

RADHAKRISHNAN PILLAI

JAICO PUBLISHING HOUSE

Ahmedabad Bangalore Bhopal Bhubaneswar Chennai
Delhi Hyderabad Kolkata Lucknow Mumbai

Published by Jaico Publishing House
A-2 Jash Chambers, 7-A Sir Phirozshah Mehta Road
Fort, Mumbai - 400 001
jaicopub@jaicobooks.com
www.jaicobooks.com

THUS SPOKE CHANAKYA

ISBN 978-93-86867-54-4

First Jaico Impression: 2018
Third Jaico Impression: 2018

Page design and layout: R. Ajith Kumar, Delhi

Printed by
Snehesh Printers
320-A, Shah & Nahar Ind. Est. A-1
Lower Parel, Mumbai - 400 013

To the Chanakya in You

INTRODUCTION

When my publisher asked me to come up with yet another book on Chanakya, it took me some time to decide on a topic. I first thought of writing about Chanakya's teachings but later changed my mind and decided to put together what I understood from his teachings.

Look at it this way, if Chanakya was alive today and wanted to share all his wisdom with us in a simple style, what would he do?

Would he write another *Kautilya's Arthashastra*? Well, my guess is that he would simplify the *Arthashastra* to suit our fast-paced generation.

Compared to Chanakya's time, we are facing issues that were unimaginable then. Our world is developing at an alarming speed. What you thought of as the latest technology is already old before you start using it. Distance is not a problem anymore; we can travel across continents in hours. Communication with anyone anywhere is possible in real time. Think of the person you want to talk to and you can connect to him from right where you are, no matter where he is in the world.

Even after all this, our major problem is time management. So much to do and so little time.

If Chanakya was around, he would understand that this generation doesn't want to spend too much time gathering wisdom. They want it quick, short, here and now.

That was the thought that made me write this book.

Thus Spoke Chanakya is made of simple one-liners explained in two paragraphs, distilled from Chanakya's insightful teachings in the *Arthashastra*. There are around 300 such one-liners that cover various subjects like leadership, time management, family, trust, productivity, etc.

All these are Chanakya's original thoughts, explained in different words, in a different time. I have just put his wisdom in simple sentences to make it easy for all of us to understand. This book has been created with a lot of thought — keeping the essence of Chanakya, yet presenting in different fashion.

In this book you will find that many ideas are repeated time and again. Please note that this is no mistake but by design. I want those ideas to be emphasized. By repeating them, I'm making sure these nuggets of wisdom get embossed inside your mind.

Also, you can use the wisdom of Chanakya in different contexts and different scenarios, as per your requirement. For instance, advice about family can be used in workplaces, because today our colleagues are our extended family members and the workplace is a home away from home. And vice versa, some ideas about the workplace can be used at home, too.

So be free to choose where and when you want to use this ancient wisdom. It works even today, guaranteed.

There are different ways of reading this book.

- Read it in one go

You can read the whole book in one sitting. There is so much to learn and yet you will be able to move from one idea to the other smoothly, because all these brilliant and profound ideas are presented as short and simple pieces. First, read it alone and then read it in a group. Discuss and discover.

- Read one verse a day

After you have read it in one go, start again. Now read one idea (verse) every day, treat it like your daily mental exercise. When you wake up in the morning, select one thought from the book; you can select it randomly, that is the beauty of this book. Read the section in detail, so that you grasp the idea in full, and think about it the whole day.

- Read it again and again

This is not a one-time read. Treat it as your companion for life. Read it again and again, till you and the book become one. I would also suggest that you start teaching these ideas to others. After all, Chanakya was a teacher.

The book is titled 'Thus Spoke Chanakya'.

Yes, he did impart these ideas.

But finally, you have to lead a life in a manner that people will look upto you and say...

"Thus spoke _____" (add your name here)

THUS SPOKE
CHANAKYA

—————

ANCIENT WISDOM FOR
DAILY INSPIRATION

♞ Political science — the ultimate discipline

Chanakya was a teacher of political science (*raja niti* or *arthashastra*). Kings themselves were his students, and many of his pupils later went on to become kings. Like many of the great teachers of the past, Chanakya also believed that *raja vidya* (knowledge of political science) is *parama vidya* (the ultimate knowledge). *Raja niti* covers all subjects, be it philosophy, spirituality, economics, law, foreign policy, military strategies, etc. The culmination of all this knowledge is *raja vidya*.

A *raja* (leader) needs to master various subjects in order to become a good leader. So if one wants to be a leader, the person has to study various disciplines. As a leader, one cannot shirk responsibility and say that he does not understand this particular subject or that. It is wise to have a good teacher like Chanakya who can advise on various subjects in one go. A good leader should be a good strategist and should have studied *raja vidya* in order to run his kingdom, or in modern context, any organization.

♞ Never go into battle alone

Chanakya was a war strategist and a military expert. His book, *Kautilya's Arthashastra*, is an excellent work on *yudh niti* (war strategies and policies). The *Arthashastra* contains 6,000 *sutras* divided into 15 books on various subjects. Out

EVEN IF YOU ARE A SMALL PLAYER AGAINST AN ENORMOUS ENEMY, DURING THE WAR, HAVE AN ALLY ON YOUR SIDE. THIS GIVES YOU MORE POWER THAN JUST MILITARY CLOUT.

of these, seven books are dedicated to warfare alone. The war tactics explained in these books can help a small kingdom protect itself from the attack of larger nations. At the same time, it can help empires retain territories from enemies.

Chanakya suggests that even if you are confident, never go into battle alone. This is the ultimate war advice from the master of battle techniques. Always take a friend along with you. Even if you are a small player against an enormous enemy, during the war, have an ally on your side. This gives you more power than just military clout. Remember, synergy is the way to win a battle. So, the next time you are in a difficult situation, call a friend and take him along to face the challenge.

♞ The four approaches — *sama, dana, bheda & danda*

Chanakya the Strategist was a simple yet profound person. He could convey his plans in just a sentence or a few words. His formulae are easy to remember and could come in handy in any situation. In his works, Chanakya provides alternative routes to reach your goal. If one method does not work, try another, and success is sure to follow.

Chanakya's four-fold policy can be applied to achieve success in anything.

- *Sama* — Discuss. One does not have to confront the opponent first. Try to get across the point.

- *Dana* — Offer financial benefits. Try to get things done through providing financial incentives to others.

- *Bheda*— Split. Divide and rule is the policy here. If things do not work out with a straight approach, create a difference of opinion in the enemy camp.

- *Danda* — Chastise. Ultimately, if nothing works, one may have to resort to harsh measures to reach the goal. However, select this route only if you must.

♞ Is punishment necessary?

Chanakya's *Arthashastra* is also known as the Book of Punishments (*danda niti*). Chanakya knew it was only because of fear of the consequences that people maintained law and order in a society. Otherwise, the law of the jungle (*matsya nyaya*) will take over, where the large fish will eat the small fish, and finally society will become dysfunctional. Therefore, to maintain peace and harmony, some penalties have to be incorporated in any institution, whether it is a country, organization or family.

When a child behaves badly, he should be reprimanded and shown the fault in his ways so that he learns the important lesson of keeping oneself under control (*mariyada*). This also instills awareness in the mind of the child. This understanding of not crossing the line is necessary to bring up a child as a responsible citizen.

♞ A leader should be like a father

In most traditional societies, the father is the head of the family. The father figure, the role model, has an important part to play in the lives of the other family members. First and foremost, his duty is to keep the household together during challenging times. Next is to care for everyone in the family — the weak, the sick, women and children, all have to be taken care of. Thus, Chanakya wants every leader to be a father figure as described in *Kautilya's Arthashastra*.

THE LOVE OF A MOTHER AND THE DISCIPLINE OF A FATHER, BOTH ARE NECESSARY FOR THE HEALTHY DEVELOPMENT OF A CHILD

But what about the mother? According to Swami Chinmayananda, "The love of a mother and the discipline of a father, both are necessary for the healthy development of a child." A leader has to make sure that he loves everyone but also disciplines them at the same time. For this, the leader has to develop the qualities of a mother — care, love and compassion. When both discipline and love are balanced, we find a great leader who inspires and brings people together.

🐎 Keep company with the wise

Satsangh is a word quite common in our Indian culture. It means 'in the company of good people'. Even Chanakya emphasizes this point in the *Arthashastra*, Book 1, Chapter 5, Association with Elders. He calls it *vridddhasanyogah*; *vriddha* means elders (by age and experience) and *sanyogah* means company. So, Chanakya advises everyone, including leaders, to keep company with wise people. The logic behind this statement is that leaders will be able to solve their problems with the help of the wise.

STUDIES SUGGEST THAT WE ARE INFLUENCED BY THE THOUGHTS OF THOSE AROUND US. THERE IS A SAYING THAT A MAN IS THE AVERAGE OF FIVE PEOPLE HE SPENDS THE MOST TIME WITH.

Studies suggest that we are influenced by the thoughts of the people around us. There is a saying that a man is the average of five people he spends the most time with. Therefore, choose your company carefully; surround yourself with wise people. Seek the advice of the intelligent in every path of your life. Read their books, watch inspiring videos about them; talk about brilliant minds and discuss about them. Make smart people and their thoughts a part of your life.

♞ Plan out your work and work out your plan

Chanakya was a master strategist. He knew what he wanted to achieve. He was crystal clear in his thinking. It is very evident in his writings that he had a plan to achieve his goals. That plan was very well executed, too. In the *Arthashastra*, there is a daily timetable for a king (Book 1, Chapter 19, Rules for the King). This particular chapter gives detailed information about the way planning was done in those days. Right from the time he woke up to when he finally went to bed at night, every minute of a ruler's life was deliberate. And Chanakya made sure that the plan was meticulously followed, too.

If you do not plan your life, you will be working for someone else who has planned out theirs in detail. Those who plan their days are in control of their lives. They are proactive and are not taken by surprise when there are sudden changes in circumstances. They also become good time managers. They do not waste their time in unnecessary things. Such people have a purpose to live for. They are self-inspired and self-motivated. They also inspire others around them with their habit of careful planning and execution.

♞ The day you start your career, plan your retirement

Chanakya recognized that nothing is permanent. Kings come and go, but good governance must last. Therefore, he trained his students to work in such a way that their work remained eternal and permanent. How? In the *Arthashastra*, he made succession planning for a king (Book 1, Chapter 18, The Conduct of a Prince) an important part of his leadership training. As a guru, Chanakya also made sure there were backup plans for every person, so that the work they began did not suffer in their absence.

When do you plan your retirement? The day you take up a job. Usually the mindset is that when you reach the end of your career, you look for someone else to take over your work (at times, you do not even want to retire, and dislike anyone else taking your place). But this is faulty thinking. It is important to train others so that even after you are gone, the work you started continues. The reality is that a nation or an organization is not dependant on any person. Probably, it will do better without you around.

♞ Be money-conscious, not money-minded

Chanakya wrote the world famous book *Kautilya's Arthashastra* that deals with wealth and money management. But fortune is a double-edged sword; it can make you wise or vicious. Chanakya suggests one should be very careful while dealing with money. Before he starts discussing the topic of economics (Book 2 of the *Arthashastra*, Activities of the Heads of Departments), he deals with the concept of self-control — *indriyajaya* (Book 1, Chapter 6, Control over the Senses). In this chapter, he states that those who deal with riches should be detached from it.

MONEY IS A RESOURCE TO BE USED, BUT CREATING WEALTH WITHOUT VALUES IS PRECARIOUS. AT THE SAME TIME, THOSE WHO FEEL MONEY IS NOT NECESSARY ARE NOT BEING PRACTICAL.

A good leader should be money-conscious. Any project or undertaking requires funds. But one should not consider monetary gain as the end objective of the project. Those who think that way are money-minded. Money is a resource to be used, but creating wealth without values is precarious. At the same time, those who feel money is not necessary are not being practical. Use money as an important tool, so you have the best means to chase your dreams. But having good tools alone does not make one a good carpenter. The qualities or the abilities of the person using the tool are equally important.

🐎 Supervise your people

Leadership is about delegating work succesfully. Chanakya deals with the topic of effective allocation in the *Arthashastra*. For that, one needs to first define the work (Book 1, Chapter 19, Rules for a King), then select the right people (Book 1, Chapter 8, *Amatya Utpatti* or Appointment of Ministers) and assign the work to them to implement it. However, the work of a leader is not over yet. From time to time, a leader needs to review the work of his subordinates to make sure it is on track. Without supervision and review, even the most efficient people become unproductive.

Try this formula with one of the projects that you are currently handling. Define the scope of the work, select the right people and hand over the work to them. Then sit back and relax. But at the end of the day, when you check on the workers, the chances are that you will be shocked. Because no one was monitoring the progress, the outcome would not have been to your liking or standard. But if you monitor and supervise the work from time to time, you will see that it is progressing at the right speed, in the right direction. Finally, regular reviews bring excellent results.

♞ Spend quality time on interviews

Many people take interviews for granted. Whenever they have someone joining their organization, they approach it like a regular process. But it is the most important activity before any new person joins a firm. You are taking a vital decision for your organization, yourself as well as the person joining, therefore, spend quality time on interviews. The right questions and quality discussions will ensure that you have the best candidate joining your team.

In the *Arthashastra*, Chanakya also stresses on the importance of selection of the genuine candidate (Book 1, Chapter 5, Association with Elders). He would not only spend good amount of time in reviewing a candidate but also regularly asked other experts to join the selection panel during an interview. An expert opinion is always good. If you select the right seed, the fruits it will bear will also be equally good.

So take your time to find the right person for the right job. Once it is done, your work becomes easy and smooth. It will lead to success in all your undertakings.

♞ Pay the best wages and pay on time

How does one decide the salary of an employee or a hired-help? Sounds impossible? Worry not, there is a way to decide on a fair compensation. According to the *Arthashastra*, "The payment of the wages was decided on the basis of work done, time spent in doing it, at the rate prevailing at the time." The way a person works and their productivity makes the salary go up or down. From time to time, as per your capacity, you need to raise the salaries of all those who work for you. Yes, people toil for their wages, but they also would like to work for the right person.

THE PAYMENT OF THE WAGES WAS DECIDED ON THE BASIS OF WORK DONE, TIME SPENT IN DOING IT, AT THE RATE PREVAILING AT THE TIME.

Therefore, while deciding the salaries of your workers, be large-hearted. Pay as per your best capability. However, do not go out of your way to pay high salaries; make sure you try to do your best when it comes to compensating your people. Also, make sure you pay on time. Paying people on time is something that cements their trust in you. It is also a mark of respect towards the other person and their contribution.

♞ Distance is a state of mind

What is the unit of measurement of distance? It is meters, miles, kilometers, etc., right? Yes, that is true from a physics standpoint. But, there is also a different way of measuring distance. It is how you perceive it. For example, to a lazy person, walking for about 200 metres could be a long walk, while for someone who is swift and fast, even a couple of kilometers is only a short distance.

Chanakya lived in an era where covering distances was not as easy as it is for our generation. There were no buses, no trains, no flights or good roads. And that makes one wonder how he managed to travel all over India (which was a much larger territory than it is today) and establish a whole empire under Chandragupta Maurya. It was possible only because he had a vision larger than himself. So if you want to be a winner, do not look at how far it is; get up and start walking. You will reach your destination soon.

♞ Look into the eyes of a person to know who he is

There is a lot of research that is being done in understanding human behaviour. And one important area is the study of body language. The human body is continuously sending messages through its actions. If you are trained to understand the various signs that are being passed on, you will be able to understand the other person easily. One of the best ways is to look into the eyes of the other person. Eyes communicate a lot nonverbally. For example, shifty eye contact means the person is guilty of something or trying to conceal something. Intense eye contact could reflect sexual attraction, anger, predatory behaviour or deception, depending on the context.

Chanakya had trained his spies in the art and science of body language — *dehvidya*. He talks about it in the *Arthashastra*, Book 4, Chapter 7, Inquest on Sudden Deaths. These spies had to understand human behaviour in order to get the information they required. The way a person stands, the look in the eyes of the person, other non-verbal clues, all were essential for a spy. Based on this information, Chanakya would then make plans and strategies to win over others. If you want to be a winner, look into the eyes of the other person, because eyes are the window to one's soul.

♞ A meeting point is a communication point

We meet our friends and acquaintances at food joints, cafes, homes, offices and other public places to interact with each other. In the olden days, people used to meet at town halls, at temples and even near wells and on river banks. These were the places where social interaction and exchanges took place.

Chanakya knew very well where all these meeting points were in his kingdom. He used these places to communicate with the citizens. (This strategy was later followed in a big way by Ashoka, the grandson of Chandragupta.) Chanakya would put up messages on huge rocks besides places like ports and highways for people to read. This method is still used in modern advertising where large billboards are hoisted on highways, near airports and railway stations, which are always full of people.

🐎 Marriage is about mutual respect

The institution of marriage is the very foundation of Indian culture. Chanakya, while shaping the great Mauryan Empire, made sure that marriage is given its due in society. The laws of marriage were clearly defined in the *Arthashastra*, Book 3, Chapter 2, Concerning Marriage. Chanakya lays down the specifics related to matrimony, like the right age for getting married, qualities to look for in a spouse, finances involved in a conjugal relationship and divorce. The most important aspect of any marriage is mutual respect among the two partners. *Prithavi Suktam* of the *Atharva Veda* from where Chanakya drew his inspiration from also mentions these aspects of nuptials.

Today we talk about women empowerment. However, in Indian culture, we always believed in giving respect to each other, irrespective of gender. Women were equally involved in all decisions made in the family. Even financial decisions were taken together. Where there is lack of mutual respect for each other among the spouses, not only the individuals but the family, too, suffers. Therefore, let us revive our traditional family values so that our next generation can draw inspiration from them.

♞ A partnership succeeds with clarity of roles and expectations

Two people cannot be equal. Each person is unique. Let us celebrate the uniqueness in every person instead of equality. This is true in partnerships, too. Chanakya knew that one cannot fight a battle alone. Friends and allies are essential to win any war. In the Saptang Model mentioned in the *Arthashastra* (*swami, amatya, janapada, durg, kosha, danda* and *mitra* constitute the seven vital organs of a state), Chanakya gives a lot of emphasis to *mitra* (friend/partner). Partnerships break due to many factors, but the most decisive of them is the ego that comes between the two partners. That has to be handled carefully.

LET THE PARTNERS DEFINE EACH OTHER'S ROLE CLEARLY. IT WILL BE BETTER TO HAVE DIFFERENCE OF OPINIONS IN THE BEGINNING OF THE PARTNERSHIP RATHER THAN AT THE END OF IT.

The next most crucial factor is the clarity of roles among the partners. If you want any partnership or association to succeed, let the partners define each other's role clearly. It will be better to have difference of opinions in the beginning of the partnership rather than at the end of it. Each person comes with certain strengths and weaknesses.

Bring your strengths into your partnerships and also be aware of your weakness. Find a partner who can balance your weaknesses. Finally, true strength lies in differences, not in similarities.

♞ Study every day

Do you know how many hours per day Chanakya wanted his students to study? For an ordinary student, it was a full day. After becoming a leader, a minimum three hours per day has to be given to studies. The *Arthashastra* defines the routine of a king in Book 1, Chapter 19, Rules for the King. In this chapter, he gives importance to *swadhyaya* or self-study on a daily basis. You may be wondering that once somebody becomes a leader/king, where is the time to study? But in reality, if you do not study every day, you will not become a good leader.

Leaders are readers. This popular saying is very crucial to any modern-day leader, too. Whichever field you belong to, be it politics, administration, industry, military, academics or even social space, studying your subject daily is a must. As nutrition and exercise are a must for a fit and healthy body, reading and studying are important for the growth of mind and intellect. Leaders have to sharpen their intellect on a daily basis. This is where *swadhyaya* comes in. After studying alone, one can also try group study. Two minds work better than a single one.

♞ Conquer yourself before you conquer the world

Chanakya wanted everyone to be a winner. But a winner is not someone who triumphs over the outside world. The real champion is the one who achieves victory over himself. The chapter on *Indriya Jaya* (Book 1, Chapter 6, Control over the Senses) is the very foundation of leadership in the *Arthashastra*. The one who wins (*jaya*) his senses (*indriya*) will be able to outshine anyone else. The most difficult person to master is oneself. If you truly achieve *indriya jaya*, the world will be at your feet.

Stephen Covey, the American educator and businessman, in his book *The 7 Habits of Highly Effective People* says that what is inside reflects outside. So work on your inner self before you work on your outer self. Your thoughts and your values will be reflected in your actions. Cleanse your inside and your actions will shine through. The real journey to success begins when you take the inner path. You discover that the secret to success is within you.

♞ Do you have a guru?

Who will show you the inner path to success? The guru. A guru is not a mere mortal being. He is not just an individual. He is an inner calling you have within yourself. It is a search that ends when God sends you a human being who guides you towards your goal. This kind of

The right combination of a teacher and student can work wonders for the student as well as for the society.

gurus is rare yet available. The real answer to the question, "Do you have a guru?" is, are you the right student? The universe operates within certain eternal laws and principles. One of them is: when the student is ready, the teacher arrives.

Chanakya was an ideal guru to Chandragupta Maurya while Chandragupta was an ideal student to Chanakya. When these two met, it was like magic. Such combinations work wonders. Whenever the right teacher and student meet, positive change takes place. This is the truth. So, how does one know who is the guru? Swami Chinmayananda used to say, "Only you will know it. An inner bell will ring and you will know that you have found your guru. The experience of finding a guru is so personal that it cannot be explained. You will know it, because you have found him."

♞ Information is the first step to success

Spies were an important part of the system that Chanakya had created for good leadership. In the *Arthashastra*, Book 1, Chapter 12, Rules for Secret Servants, he refers to the kind of spies that a government should have. Spies gather information for the leader. Based on this information, the leader takes his decisions. Being informed is necessary for making a plan towards your goal. Also just information is not enough. One should know how to sort through all the data gathered, because all of it may not be correct.

SPIES GATHER INFORMATION FOR THE LEADER. BASED ON THIS INFORMATION, THE LEADER TAKES HIS DECISIONS. BEING INFORMED IS NECESSARY FOR MAKING A FOOL-PROOF PLAN TOWARDS YOUR GOAL.

Today there are various methods to gather information, be it the newspapers, the internet or various news channels. However, with an overload of information, one can also get confused. Once we know how to handle the information available, we can work towards our goals. For example, if you want to win an Olympic medal in a particular category, you need to know the game, other players, rules, etc., well. With that, you can slowly start planning for success. Remember, the first step is information, next is strategy and then comes hard work.

🐎 Rules are important

You will find rules and regulations everywhere, be it a game, an organization or a country. These rules are important to keep things going in the right track. Chanakya wanted his country to be governed very well. For that, he wrote the *Arthashastra*, which is like a guidebook for good governance. He clearly defines rules and regulations for every person in every area, be it collecting the taxes, land acquisitions, taking over an enemy fort, paying salaries or even marriages. Rules help to maintain order. Rules direct you towards what is right and help you avoid what is wrong.

Ignorance of the law does not allow you to break the law. Therefore, it is important to study the laws beforehand. For instance, if you join any organization, there is an orientation programme for new employees. This is to inform the newcomer what the existing systems are, what is allowed and not allowed, etc. This will help the new employee understand the freedom and the limits given to every person. Know the rules well so that you can excel at your job.

🐎 Wealth is in the countryside

How does one become wealthy? By knowing the source of wealth. Chanakya says in the *Arthashastra*, Book 7, Chapter 14, Recoupment of Powers Become Weak, "Wealth and power comes from the countryside, which is the source of all activities." If you take any country, you will find that all their natural resources are in the rural areas; the maximum population of any nation lives in the countryside. It is important for a king to focus on the rural areas of his kingdom. An efficient leader knows that in the capital (*rajdhani*), only trading activity happens. But the real wealth creation takes place in the countryside. One needs to connect the urban and the rural to amass wealth.

M. K. Gandhi had said that the soul of India lives in its villages. It is true for every country. Even though we have become a modernized, technologically empowered society, the countryside is where we need to focus. From time to time, visit the villages and keep an eye on the rich resources many are not aware of. Man will always be connected with nature. We still need agriculture for our basic survival. So, connect with nature in the countryside where the real source of wealth is.

♞ Be the future

Think fast, think ahead. Most of us are only thinking to get ahead of the person next to us. But winners know that we need to be the future. 'Create the future' is the mantra for success. Book 2 of the *Arthashastra* deals with economic activities and interestingly, Chanakya starts the first chapter with the idea of creating new villages. It was important for Chanakya to think about modern and new activities. Thus, by creating a new village and a new ecosystem, he was ushering in creativity and thereby finding progress and growth.

LET OTHERS DO WHAT THEY ARE DOING WHILE YOU SLOWLY START WORKING ON A DIFFERENT PATH ALL TOGETHER. BE THE FUTURE, BE THE NEXT. TRY AND EXPERIMENT WITH SOMETHING DIFFERENT.

Most of us compare ourselves with others and want to get ahead of them. Change the strategy. Let others do what they are doing while you slowly start working on a different path all together. Try and experiment with something different. Most companies that do well have research and development (R&D) departments. They keep innovating and working towards new products and services. Instead of chasing the past, be the future, be the next big thing.

♞ Spend quality time thinking

A leader should be a thinker first. Chanakya had developed a science and art of thinking named *aanvikshiki*. He called it *'pradeep sarva viyanaamah'* — the lamp of all sciences. *Aanvikshiki* is supposed to make one proficient in thought, speech and action. It is only because of the power of mind that human beings have marched ahead of other species. Therefore, if we want to progress further, we need to spend quality time with ourselves, spend more time thinking.

Thinking is not just sitting somewhere and doing nothing. Most of us even confuse it with worrying. It is a scientific and structured process. One needs to allocate some time only for thinking, one hour a day, and it can bring a sea of change to the quality of our lives. Like we give importance to the right type of food for the body, let us also give nourishment to our mind with right thoughts. Contemplating makes us go to the next level; open the doors to a whole new world of possibilities.

♞ Continuous thinking leads to success

Thinking once or twice about your dreams and goals is not enough to reach the pinnacle of success. Any accomplishment is a process, so continue to think from various angles, on various possibilities of how you can attain what you want. Chanakya taught Chandragupta how to reason during his training and he wanted the king to deliberate every day about his plans for the kingdom. In the *Arthashastra*, he allocates time for the king to be alone and spend time reflecting and pondering over various issues concerning the welfare of his subjects. It is only through continuous thinking that one develops insights. These insights are very important for a leader to cultivate good decision-making skills.

Stay on a problem longer than the others. This is the way to success. When you look at a problem initially, you tend to look at it superficially. But as you keep analyzing further, you will discover various new dimensions and vistas. New perspectives will give you new possibilities. And as you keep working deeper, you will develop a subtle intellect that will open up a new world. From this kind of deep and broad thinking, you will emerge an expert who will redefine the whole field (whichever field you are working on), today and forever.

🐎 Invest in good infrastructure

In the Saptanga Model of governance, Chanakya gives a lot of emphasis to *durga*, the fort. It is among the most important focus areas for a king. Without a sturdy fort, a kingdom will not be able to function safely. In the olden days, cities used to have forts surrounding them, with an ecosystem of their own. The habitation inside the fort consisted of excellent infrastructure — houses, water reservoirs, the king's palace, etc. Such good infrastructure was meant to make the king look powerful in the eyes of both internal and external enemies.

Even in the modern days we should give utmost importance to our '*durga*'. Your immediate environment is your fort, your stronghold, so invest in good infrastructure at your home and work places. Your house or office maybe small, but it can be beautiful and efficient. Today we require both physical and digital infrastructure for smooth functioning. Therefore, make sure it is world-class, but within your budget. It is a myth that good infrastructure requires heavy funding and big budgets. It is always the vision of the leader that makes the infrastructure state-of-the-art.

🐎 Make documentation a habit

When embark on a project, plan it, do it, record it — this is the golden principle to follow. While Chanakya gave a lot of importance to planning and implementation, he also made sure everything was properly recorded. In the *Arthashastra*, government records are given prime importance and considered as national wealth. In fact, it was mandatory for the king to go through all the previous records of the kingdom

WHILE CHANAKYA GAVE A LOT OF IMPORTANCE TO PLANNING AND IMPLEMENTATION, HE ALSO MADE SURE EVERYTHING WAS PROPERLY RECORDED. IN THE *ARTHASHASTRA*, GOVERNMENT RECORDS ARE CONSIDERED AS NATIONAL WEALTH.

during his training period. One will be able to see the future of a kingdom or an organization through its past.

Make record keeping and documentation a habit. This habit in the initial days may feel very mechanical and boring. But as you progress, you will start realizing the importance of this activity suggested in the *Arthashastra*. This goes on to build your intellectual capital and intellectual property. Anytime you want to refer to it, it is available on your fingertips.

♘ Write a book

If Chanakya had not written the *Arthashastra*, we would have lost the wealth of knowledge that he had created. According to Chanakya, work is important, but documenting the same is equally vital. Therefore, he made sure that the government machinery created reports, so that they can be used by the future kings and ministers for reference.

Similarly, every individual should write a book. Do not worry about who will read your book. The book is not necessarily for others; writing is a process of self-reflection. When you write a book, you will be compelled to look back to check what were the reasons for your successes and failures. This way, you will learn from your mistakes and will not repeat it in the future. Also, those who read your book eventually, even if it is just one person, will gather something relevant and useful from your writings. Thus, you will be passing on the knowledge and wisdom from one generation to another.

♞ Be ready with alternatives

If you are stuck in life, you need to think a way out of the problem. There could be many alternative solutions to one problem. Remember the famous four alternative strategies of Chanakya: *sama, dana, bheda* and *danda*? This is the classic example for having substitute options. If one way does not work, try another. If that too does not work, there could be a third method. Stop not till your goal is achieved. Chanakya suggests the game of chess (called *chaturanga* in the *Arthashastra*) for developing this ability of alternative thinking, so that we are not stuck with any problem, rather we become a solution to any problem.

Let us not be boring when it comes to thinking. Innovation is a limitless activity. And it all begins with the mind. So stretch your mental limits. Think out of the box, think beyond the box and even question whether there is any box at all. Is the box real or only a mental block? At times you may discover that what you started seeing as a hitch is usually not the real problem. The real problem is in the mind. So play with your own mind to get it to obey you.

◢ Stop thinking

Chanakya was a strategist, he was a planner. A competent tactician knows that there are some things beyond the human intellect. Therefore, in order to think better, from time to time, we need to stop thinking. In the *Arthashastra*, Chanakya has included short breaks from time to time in the routine of the king. Only when the leader takes breaks can he rejuvenate and rejoin the team with new ideas and plans. So give yourself a 'thinking break' to become a better leader.

Nature has cycles of day and night. During the day everyone works hard while at night we are supposed to rest and sleep. This routine is perfectly followed by other species as well. In our case, with the invention of electricity, the distinction between day and night is almost erased. We do not follow the natural order anymore. But it is important to rest well. So, let us follow the cycle of work and rest properly. Work hard and rest well today so that we can work harder tomorrow.

◢ A leader lives to serve others

"*Praja sukhe sukham rajnah,*" says the *Arthashastra*, Book 1, Chapter 19, Verse 34. It means, in the happiness of the subjects lies the happiness of the king. This is the crux of leadership according to Chanakya. There may be hundreds of theories out there about how to become a leader. But finally, the right attitude of a person determines whether he is an able leader or not, and the topmost quality of a leader is his willingness to serve others. Therefore, Chanakya says that the leader lives to serve others.

If you are a leader or aspire to become one, remember that it is not an easy path. The journey is full of challenges. There will be times when people will not even understand you or your vision. Your life will be full of sacrifices and service. You must have a large heart to love all and a broad shoulder to handle all the responsibilities. Therefore, be ready to take up a life that is fully dedicated to the welfare of others. With such an attitude, one will be able to climb to the pinnacles of leadership.

♞ Think about the happiness and wellbeing of your people

Chanakya clearly differentiates between happiness and wellbeing. Happiness is 'sukha', while Wellbeing is 'hita'. All that makes you happy may not necessarily be good for you. Chocolates may make you happy, but if you are diabetic, then it is poison for you. Similarly, all that is for your wellbeing may not make you happy. For instance, if you are ill, a doctor may give you an injection to treat you. But the prick of the needle is painful and may leave you with some discomfort.

A leader therefore has to think about sukha and hita of his people. The Arthashatra, Book 1, Chapter 19, Verse 34, says, "Prajanam cha hite hitam." In the wellbeing of the people is his own wellbeing. Therefore, a good leader knows to balance happiness and wellbeing. For a parent, welfare of his children is his utmost priority. If you are in a leadership position, you are like a parent to your colleagues and subordinates, and you may have to take some tough calls, which may not be liked by the majority. Yet, the intention behind your decision should be their benefit in the long run, even if it is causing some temporary discomfort.

♘ Plan for the worst-case scenario

Chanakya starts the *Arthashastra* with an interesting prayer: *Om Namah Sukra Bhrashaspati Abhyam* — salutations to the great gurus Shukracharya and Brahaspati. Shukracharya was the guru of the Rakshasas (demons) while Bhrahaspati was the guru of the Devas (gods). Instead of taking a stand on who is right and who is wrong, Chanakya offers obeisance to both the teachers. Interestingly, both these sages were experts in their own style of warfare.

WHILE PLANNING ANYTHING, THE KEY IS TO LOOK AT ALL THE ALTERNATIVE VIEWS PRESENTED TO YOU. RESPECT AND WELCOME ALL OPINIONS. START BY LOOKING AT THE WORST-CASE SCENARIO.

While planning anything, the key is to look at all the alternative views presented to you. Respect and welcome all opinions. Start by looking at the worst-case scenario. What if the project does not take off? What if all resources get exhausted mid way? This is not negative thinking, but practical thinking. This does not mean that you will fail or you are preparing to fail. It is preparing your mind to be open to all possibilities. When you plan this way, your mind will tell you how not to fail.

♞ Plan for the best-case scenario

Like you prepared yourself for the worst-case scenario, prepare for the best-case scenario, too. What if you win? What if you become successful? This way, your mind will garner positive thoughts and will develop self-confidence. Now, in between failure and success lies reality. Chanakya is known as a practical thinker. When you look at both possibilities, you get a balanced view. Your mind becomes calm and you are able to see all the problems clearly. One need not be pessimistic or optimistic, one needs to be realistic. That is the real route to success.

While taking decisions in life, you need to consider both success and failure. There are random risk takers, but practical people take calculated risks. A risky move that is assessed beforehand gives you a backup plan, an option to fall back on, in case something goes wrong along the way. Otherwise, if you take risks based only on emotions, there is a higher chance of failure. You may have sentiments but do not become sentimental. Be sensitive but also be sensible.

♞ Conflict should be the last option

Who likes a war? War means destruction; it leads to loss of lives and property. During a war, the whole society goes through turmoil, and therefore, war should be avoided as much as possible. Contrary to popular belief, Chanakya was against unnecessary conflict.

Always negotiate for peace and a win-win opportunity. Therefore, Chanakya gives utmost importance to the envoys in the *Arthashastra*, Book 1, Chapter 16, Rules for the Envoy). The ambassador or the envoy of a country plays a very crucial role in avoiding wars with the host countries. In the *Mahabharata*, before the war, Krishna had gone to the Kauravas as a *shantidoot* (messenger of peace). Behind every one war that happened in history there were thousands of such potential disasters defused by intelligent peacekeepers.

♞ Be ready to defend yourself

India is known to be a peace-loving nation. We were always a strong and powerful nation and we never misused our military strength. However, we also defended our territories when it was necessary. But we never had the need to invade any other nation as we are self-sufficient. Nature has blessed us with plenty of resources. And if someone unnecessarily troubled us, we have the means to defend ourselves, too.

Book 7, Chapter 5 of the *Arthashatra* deals with a king ready to attack. Chanakya would carefully study the enemy, look at his strengths and weaknesses and plan his moves according to the given circumstances. When Chanakya got involved a war, he made sure that his side won, every time.

♞ Be ready to be confronted

A leader should be alert about the threats to his position at all times. Thinking that the whole world is good just like you is stupidity. Your vision and ideas will be challenged. In today's digital world, no view or plan goes unchallenged and people are more aware of the workings of organizations and government machineries than ever before. Public opinion can turn any moment and when it happens, it can fell large trees in a matter of seconds, which was impossible before.

Chanakya was prepared against the attacks of enemies at all times. This does not mean he was looking for a fight. But if someone was to attack his kingdom, he was ready to defend it. That is why nations have defence forces. The army of a nation is ever alert and ready, in case some neighbour tries to invade. Therefore, Chanakya suggests investing in the

IN TODAY'S DIGITAL WORLD, NO VIEW OR PLAN GOES UNCHALLENGED AND PEOPLE ARE MORE AWARE OF THE WORKINGS OF ORGANIZATIONS AND GOVERNMENT MACHINERIES THAN EVER BEFORE.

defence systems, which have to be world-class. The same way, a leader should be prepared with his explanations to anyone who confronts his ideas.

♞ Help your friends in need

'A friend in need is a friend indeed', goes the famous saying. Human beings are social animals, so we require help from our friends. But we also need to help those friends in their need. Therefore, to have good friends, begin by being a good friend first.

In the Saptanga Model of the *Arthashastra*, Chanakya underlines that a *mitra* (ally/friend) is a very basic and essential part of creating a mighty kingdom. One could be the most powerful king, and yet he will require an ally to keep himself going strong during a war. Keeping this in mind, a powerful king sometimes had to help a weaker king during some calamity or difficult circumstances so that the favour is returned when necessary.

♞ Either you win as a team or succumb as individuals

Those who fight their challenges alone are lonely people. Strength comes from being together. Therefore, the best way to tackle a challenge or an obstacle is to go at it as a team.

When you have a team, your problems reduce in size, as you have the support of other team members. You could be the strongest person around, yet as an individual, you can be easily beaten. However, a team is a talent pool, and together, you can cover for each other's weaknesses.

When Alexander the Great came to invade, India was divided into 16 regional kingdoms. Each of them were constantly fighting with each other. For the enemy, it was a strategic advantage, as these small kingdoms could be easily defeated, one by one. But Chanakya was very clever. He united all of them and defeated Alexander. He knew the power of unity. When the enemy tried the method of divide and rule, Chanakya believed in the 'united we stand' strategy.

♞ Leadership is about winning the ego

Our mind is our best friend and our biggest enemy. Therefore, winning over the mind is very important. How does one do that? By controlling the senses is the answer. Chanakya called this self-control '*indriyajaya*'. One has to realize that controlling mind is not an easy job, it is a lifelong endeavour. Yet, it will lead to having a hold over one's ego (*ahankaar*), the first step towards becoming a great leader.

Even great leaders fall from grace when they operate out of their egos. A self-centered approach to a small issue can lead to the downfall of a kingdom, even. So, get a grip on your ego and you can rule the whole world. Chanakya also gives various examples in the *Arthashastra* of those kings in the past who were destroyed due to their egos and those who have successful reigns as they managed to keep their emotions under control.

🐎 A leader has to manage others' ego

Once a leader was asked what his greatest challenge was. He replied by saying that he considered managing the egos of his team members who kept fighting against each other the toughest part. It is true that human nature is about constant jealousy, hatred and anger. However, the same human beings also display other qualities like love, compassion and kindness. The journey of life is about evolving from the basic negative tendencies to the higher qualities inside us.

A LEADER HAS TO BE SPIRITUAL IN NATURE. WITH PATIENCE AND PRACTICE, ONE CAN ACQUIRE *RISHI*-LIKE QUALITIES AND BECOME A HIGHLY-EVOLVED PERSON SPIRITUALLY. THIS IS ONLY POSSIBLE WHEN YOU BECOME EGO-FREE.

It is a leader's responsibility to guide others towards these gentle human qualities. Therefore, a leader has to be spiritual in nature. This is why Chanakya defines an ideal leader as '*Rajarishi*' or 'a sage-like king' in the *Arthashastra*, Book 1, Chapter 3, The Life of a Sage-like King. With patience and practice, one can acquire *rishi*-like qualities and become a highly-evolved person spiritually. This is only possible when you become ego-free, and such a person will not find it difficult to manage other people's ego wars.

❧ Does war lead to peace?

The ultimate aim of war is not victory, it is peace. Take a closer look at the history of wars and you will come to realize that whether it is between kingdoms, countries or mythical beings, wars always start off with a minor issue between two people. Slowly it becomes an ego issue, a power game. As more and more people get involved, the situation worsens and soon a war is looming in the horizon.

WHEN THINGS CANNOT BE SOLVED WITH DISCUSSIONS AND DELIBERATIONS, IT FINALLY LEADS TO A WAR. CHANAKYA UNDERSTOOD THIS PSYCHOLOGY OF HUMAN BEINGS

When things cannot be solved with discussions and deliberations, it finally leads to a war. Chanakya understood this psychology of human beings. And therefore, he came up with the four-fold strategy to get things under control — *sama* (peacefully solve the issue), *dana* (offer a compensation), *bheda* (divide and rule) and *danda* (punishment). After trying the first three methods to resolve an issue, if nothing works, one may have to resort to punishment (*danda*) to bring back social order and peace within the society. So after a confrontation, peace follows.

♞ Be neutral in your approach

Most of us react rather than respond to people and situations. Reaction is impulsive and short-sighted. Whenever you face any challenging situation, you have a chance to stop, take a pause, analyze the situation and then take the next step. But for that, one needs to develop two qualities — a neutral approach to everything around and the second is to think strategically.

Chanakya wanted his students to develop a state of mind that was neutral in every given situation. *"Aanvikshiki keeps the mind steady in adversity and prosperity,"* says the *Arthashastra*, Book 1, Chapter 2, Verse 11. *Aanvikshiki* is very much the foundation of right thinking. However, being neutral does not mean to be like a vegetable, in a dead state. In this state, one appears to be calm outside but his mind is alive and active inside. Thinking and analyzing every situation without bias, a person achieves clarity of thought and action.

♞ Do not try to change others

We believe that we are perfect and the world needs to be improved. Most social workers suffer from frustration and dejection because they do not see their efforts bearing fruits on a large scale. One should serve others but also remember that the world will remain the same. Do your duty but do not expect others to recognize your work. If they do, consider it as a bonus. It is better to change ourselves than change others.

Chanakya goes one step further. According to him, a king should know that the world is made of different types of people and no one is useless. But finding the right person for the right job is real leadership. In the *Arthashastra*, Book 1, Chapter 8, Appointment of Ministers, Chanakya looks out for ideal ministers. However, he says that if you do not find the ideal person, it does not matter; you can use whoever is the best according to their capability and capacity. So, instead of changing the people around you, try to use their strengths for the benefit of all. Swami Chinmayananda used to say, "Youth are not useless, they are used less. Youth are not careless, they are cared (for) less."

A KING SHOULD KNOW THAT THE WORLD IS MADE OF DIFFERENT TYPES OF PEOPLE AND NO ONE IS USELESS. BUT FINDING THE RIGHT PERSON FOR THE RIGHT JOB IS REAL LEADERSHIP.

♞ Your territory is your advantage

One of the key factors for winning a battle is the location of the war. If you are playing in your home ground, your chances of victory are high. You know your area well, the location is familiar to you; outsiders may take ages to figure it out. Plus, the locals may know you well, so they always have a soft corner for you. This could be a reason why the Indian cricket team wins most home matches and that is mostly true for all such sporting events.

Therefore, Chanakya's advice is to get the enemy into your territory to fight the battle. This way, you will have a strategic advantage over the enemy. There is a famous Hindi saying, "*Apni gali mein kutta bhi sher hota hai.*" Even a dog is king in his area. Therefore, in the war books of the *Arthashastra* (Books 6-14), Chanakya gives high importance to the setting up of the battlefield and its location. To outsmart your enemy, challenge him in your area of expertise.

♞ The weapon of diplomacy

There are many types of weapons. Some have forms — guns, missiles, tanks, etc. But some weapons are strategic; they exist only in the minds of the leaders. There is a saying, "Battles are not fought in the battlefield but in the minds of the generals." Apart from army generals, there are many great minds who are a crucial part of a war. These are the envoys and diplomats who use mental strategies to win a war.

Diplomacy is a great weapon. The highly-trained Foreign Service officers of any country use negotiation to win a situation in their country's favour. In the *Arthashastra*, Chanakya dedicates a whole chapter to these diplomatic missions; Book 12, Chapter 1, The Mission of the Envoy. Similarly, today most countries try to avoid direct warfare but are keen to solve their issues with other countries through an alternative route of discussion, deliberation and through economic policies. So using envoys to win a war is a strategy tried even by Chanakya.

Diplomacy is a great weapon used by envoys to avoid direct warfare and solve issues with other countries.

♞ Leaders work with other leaders

Many believe that it is lonely at the top. But the world does not have just one organization or one government; there are many peaks, not just one. So if you are somebody sitting on a peak, look around, and you will notice a few others on nearby peaks. They are also leaders like you, sitting at the top and taking care of everything. So, what should a leader do when he feels lonely and bored? Try and work with other leaders. Though different leaders may be leading different kingdoms, they could be facing similar problems. Together, you can come up with solutions for these problems.

The concept of *mitra* (ally/friend) is commonly discussed across the *Arthashastra*. This *mitra* should be your philosopher and guide. He should be easily approachable and not selfish. Leaders working with other like-minded leaders are always beneficial to both parties. There are times in life when you require a hand to hold to cross turbulent waters. Having an ally of your same stature is in your own interest.

♞ Advisors can make or break you

Be careful from whom you receive advice. Choose your friends and advisors carefully. Most of the times people are not sure whom to take advice from, especially when they are facing a problem. During stressful situations, with many people offering their opinions, it is difficult to choose whom to listen to and what to discard. Remember, there is

DURING STRESSFUL SITUATIONS, WITH MANY PEOPLE OFFERING OPINIONS, IT IS DIFFICULT TO CHOOSE WHOM TO LISTEN TO AND WHAT TO DISCARD. THERE IS A BIG DIFFERENCE BETWEEN AN OPINION AND ADVICE.

a big difference between an opinion and advice. Learn to differentiate between the two.

In the *Arthashastra*, you can find quite a few places where Chanakya advices on advisors. Book 1, Chapter 9, Appointment of Councilors and Chaplains, is one of them. He used to critically evaluate every potential candidate for long-term advisor positions. Since their main job is to help the king take strategic decisions, such think tanks were the backbone of a king's team. This applies to modern-day leaders, too. So choose your advisors carefully.

♞ Convince the leader first

There are many ways of getting something done. The one that works fastest is the top-down approach. Once you convince the leader or manager in charge about what needs to be done, others just follow. Leaders have the power to influence everyone under them. So, instead of trying to beat around the bush, try to get your ideas to the top first. However, getting to the leader to present your ideas could be difficult. But once you have their support, your work will get done in a jiffy. So, try and put all your efforts into making sure you get the attention and participation of the leaders first.

However, do not forget that getting the support of the leader is not good enough. Those people who are right below the leader also wield power. They are the ones responsible for getting the job done and making sure it is executed well. The boss (*swami*) and his confidant (*amatya*), both are important to get the work done, according to Chanakya. Nevertheless, it starts with the leader at the top.

🐴 Strike at the top first

A good war strategy is figuring out who the most important person, the pillar, of your enemy troupe is and then narrowing down the attack to just that person. If you manage to knock the leader down, you have practically won the war. So, if you are ever in a situation where confrontation is unavoidable, have it directly with the leader or the person with maximum power. Once the leader is tackled, his whole team will follow suit. This is the easiest way to achieve victory in any situation.

But this is not easy. Attacking the top requires solid thinking and good planning. Chanakya knew how to do just that. Therefore, he always gathered information first. After that, he gauged who the main enemy is, his strengths and weaknesses, and devised plans to attack the core at the right time. He kept himself well-informed through his spies and intelligent networks. He has detailed his strategies in the *Arthashastra*, Book 4, Chapter 9, Keeping a Watch Over the Departments. He planned his attacks in such a way that the leader is taken down in the very first move itself — a guaranteed victory!

♞ Be a part of the system before you change it

People are unhappy about the way events are unfolding around them today, be it bad infrastructure, poor economy, atrocities against women and children, corrupt leaders and what have you. Everyone wants change. But no one wants to take the responsibility for that change. We are used to playing the blame game. We curse the leaders, the government officials and everyone else around. But when it comes to doing something about it, nobody wants to take the ownership. Chanakya was not that kind of a person. He was not the one to sit back and dole out armchair criticism. Instead, he got into the system and created the change he wanted.

WE ARE USED TO PLAYING THE BLAME GAME. WE CURSE THE LEADERS, THE OFFICIALS AND EVERYONE ELSE. BUT WHEN IT COMES TO DOING SOMETHING ABOUT IT, NOBODY WANTS TO TAKE THE OWNERSHIP.

His life is a good example of how he influenced change. He saw a bad leader (King Dhanananda), he noticed that things are not going the right way. He tried to advise the king and his entourage. But when things did not work out, he decided to get into the game and become the game changer. He created a new army of his students. He waged a war against the king and replaced Dhanananda with his own student Chandragupta, thus becoming a kingmaker. He also waged a war against Alexander the Great and defeated him when he came to conquer India. As Gandhi said, "Be the change you wish to see in the world."

♞ Understanding leads to change

Before change comes understanding. Change does not happen overnight; it is never a quick fix. Therefore, only when you study something in depth can you create the positive change you want. In the same way, Chanakya first studied the prevailing system of governance the kingdoms of India followed during his time. He tried to understand the issues that plagued the old system and come up with a plan that would be acceptable for all.

CHANAKYA TRIED TO UNDERSTAND THE ISSUES THAT PLAGUED THE OLD SYSTEM AND COME UP WITH A PLAN THAT WOULD BE ACCEPTABLE FOR ALL.

Even while writing the *Arthashastra*, Chanakya studied the previous *Arthashastras* (Yes, there were at least 14 other *Arthashastras* before Chanakya wrote his own) to understand the history of running effective kingdoms. Then he slowly started charting his own system and *Kautilya's Arthashastra* was born. Only when you understand an issue in depth will you be able to come up with a solution.

♞ Stop. Think. Proceed

In the long run, short breaks matter. Those who run marathons and cross-country races know this principle very well. Without breaks one will not be able to gather the required energy to proceed. This rule applies for everything we do in life. Work hard for success, but if you are not able to take regular breaks, you will lose direction and forget the main objective itself. Chanakya encouraged his students to stop whatever they are doing from time to time and review their progress. He wanted his students to think about how much they have achieved, how far they have to go, how effectively they can reach their goal, and only then proceed.

In the chapter on auditing (The *Arthashastra*, Book 2, Chapter 7), Chanakya talks about daily, weekly, monthly, quarterly, half-yearly and yearly reviews. This is directly practiced in the accounting process. However, he suggests such reviews even in the routine of a king.

Make sure your breaks are used for analysis and contemplation. Chanakya knew that a break is not a stop; it is just a pause before starting again, with renewed vigour.

♞ Delayed victory is not defeat

The bow and arrow are interdependent on each other. Without the bow, the arrow cannot get the lift it requires to hit the target. While, the arrow without the bow is useless. But, remember, the arrow has to bend a little and surrender to the bow to give it the momentum it requires to proceed towards its target. Also the bow has to let go the arrow after giving its full strength. This is true in war, too. Losing a battle is not losing the war.

Chanakya believed that even if we lose sometimes it does not mean that we have lost forever. We can get up, take the help of a supportive friend and attack the enemy/problem again. Book 7, Chapter 2, of the *Arthashastra* talks about a defeated king getting ready again to attack. Do not accept defeat. Even if victory comes late, it is still victory. Successful people are successful and at the top of their game because they did not give up at the face of failure. Persist and become successful in the long run.

🐎 Keep your key people happy

A king's entourage consists of various individuals, but the most important are his ministers and advisors. It is essential to keep them happy. If they are happy, they will be committed to the king. Otherwise, there is a chance of them betraying the king and the kingdom. Even in the most difficult circumstances, it is the people closest to you who will help you out of it. For example, in the Mahabharata war, many great warriors supported Duryodhana even though he was unjust to the Pandavas because he took great care of them and made them feel important.

If you go through the *Arthashastra*, you will find that the salaries of the *amatyas*, *mantris* (ministers), *raja guru*, *raja purohit*, etc., are of the highest order. They were taken care of very well, provided with all the required amenities so that their minds stay focused. When their minds are on the job, they will surely work without distraction and produce the required results. Therefore, your success depends on the happiness of the key people who work for you. After all, they do your job for you.

♞ Provide arms before you send your soldiers to war

It is very easy for the commander of an army to issue orders to attack the enemy. However, if his men go to the battle without the right strategy and weapons, they are sure to be defeated. It is a battlefield out there, so make sure you provide the right tools and training to your teammates before you ask them to complete a project on time or pitch a product. Excellent resources are very important, whether in a war or in an organization. With top-notch resources and a never-say-die spirit, any team will succeed. This is why Chanakya always made sure that Chandragupta's soldiers had access to world-class weapons.

The kind of weapons that were required by an army is clearly mentioned in the *Arthashastra*, Book 2, Chapter 15, The Superintendent of the Magazine, and it clearly shows that Chanakya knew the science of weapons well. But let us remember that arms alone are not enough, the person using them also matters. Therefore, training in weapons and preparing the person to use those weapons effectively are equally important. When you have the right man, machinery and the right strategy, no one can stop you.

♞ Do secret practices help?

There are many secret practices called *guhya vidya* mentioned in the *Arthashastra* (Book 14, chapter related to secret practices). Chanakya used these secret, occult practices to defeat enemies. You can argue that all this is mere superstition and blind faith. Some may even think of these methods as black magic. According to Chanakya, these secret practices are not to be revealed to anyone and everyone. Only the matured, ready student (*adhikari*) gets this knowledge through his teacher.

Certain Vedic mantras and hymns can be found in the *Arthashastra* that invoke certain deities and gods who have the powers to annihilate the enemy. In other ancient scriptures, there are stories of sages and kings acquiring divine weapons through strict penance (*tapas*) for protection or in order to destroy their enemies.

♞ Do your best and leave the rest

"Do your best and leave the rest," is Swami Chinmayananda's famous quote. One cannot do everything but everyone

can do something. And knowing what we can do and what
we cannot, is wisdom. Chanakya, as a master strategist,
was also aware that in spite of excellent planning, certain
things can still go wrong. So, do we sit lazily believing that
everything is pre-destined? No, it is important to do your
best first.

After doing our best we should allow nature to take its own
course. The *Bhagavad Gita* describes the philosophy of
Karma Yoga on the same lines. The *Gita* says, "*Kam karo,
phal ki chinta mat karo.*" Do your part and do not worry
about the result. You will get the results, but at its own pace.
Chanakya was a *karma yogi* by practice. He worked with
detachment and with a higher purpose. He knew that one
has to make certain things happen while some others need
to happen on their own.

♞ Test a person's integrity before you trust him

Some of us trust people blindly and then get into trouble
because of it. Each one of us has had a past experience
where we found that trusting someone had landed us in
trouble. So do we not trust people anymore? Do we just
remain doubting everyone around? That is not the solution.
We need to trust people, but after testing their integrity,
honesty and values in life.

In the *Arthashastra*, Chanakya discusses many such tests.
According to the book, the three major tests are the test of

piety, test of material gain and test of lust (Book 1, Chapter 10). These three are the pillars on which the foundation of trust stands. Only after conducting these tests did Chanakya trust people. During the testing period, he kept a close watch over those he wanted in the core team of Chandragupta Maurya. A leader's entourage should always be trustworthy.

🐎 Appoint only the right people in your core team

Even though you have thousands of people in your organization, your core team is the most important among them all. So, it is vital for a leader to select his own team. For this, you may take the help of others, but the final call should be yours.

There are many qualities you must look for when selecting your core team. The whole list of qualities is listed in the *Arthashastra*. You may not get everything you want in your key people, but choosing the right people for the right kind of roles is important. *"From the capacity for doing work is the ability of the person judged. And in accordance with the ability, by suitably distributing rank among ministers and assigning place*

> IT IS VITAL FOR A LEADER TO SELECT HIS OWN TEAM. YOU MAY NOT GET EVERYTHING YOU WANT IN YOUR KEY PEOPLE, BUT CHOOSING THE RIGHT PEOPLE IS IMPORTANT.

time and work to them he should appoint all the ministers,"
says the *Arthashastra*, Book 1, Chapter 8, Verse 29. A
successful leader is the one who has the ability to pick the
right people to assist him in his endeavours.

♞ Keep watch over enemies and also friends

Be alert and vigilant about both your enemies and your
friends. The whole spying and information network of
Chanakya was to gather news from every nook and corner
of Magadha and even from neighbouring countries.

According to the *Arthashastra*, threats to a king are of three
kinds — directly perceived, unperceived and inferred. Your
enemies are planning their moves against you, so keep a
watch over them. Your friends may not tell their problems
to you. So, you need to make sure that you understand their
troubles and solve them to the best of your capacity, so as
to not make your friends bitter and turn against you. Real
friends will know if there is a problem even without it being
communicated. So the Chanakya system is to continuously
watch everyone, all the time.

♞ Change your strategy with time

Life is about adjusting to constant change. With changing
times, the way you work also has to change. The involvement

of technology has become a very essential part of any activity these days. Without an active social media strategy, no good marketing plan will succeed today. A few years ago, social media was not that important. Therefore, when times change, change your approach.

Ashoka was a great emperor. He was the grandson of Chandragupta Maurya, whom Chanakya had made the emperor of united India. While Chanakya trained both Chandragupta and Ashoka, the strategies he taught them were quite different. As the times changed, the lessons also had to change. With Chandragupta, the focus was on defeating the enemies through warfare; Ashoka was trained to use diplomacy more than confrontation. Ashoka's last war was at Kalinga, and then he took a different route to win over the world, the route of peace.

WITHOUT AN ACTIVE SOCIAL MEDIA STRATEGY, NO GOOD MARKETING PLAN WILL SUCCEED TODAY. A FEW YEARS AGO, SOCIAL MEDIA WAS NOT THAT IMPORTANT. THEREFORE, WHEN TIMES CHANGE, CHANGE YOUR APPROACH.

♞ Everyone is not successful everywhere

Everyone is not successful everywhere but there are successful people everywhere. The trick is to understand where you will be successful and associate with successful people in other areas. For instance, if you are talented in music, you can be a successful musician. But you may not be so good in sports. So, you should focus on music as a path to success in life. If you still love sports, associate with someone who is a successful sportsman. This way you will have the best of both worlds.

In the *Rajamandala* Theory mentioned in Book 6 of the *Arthashastra*, Chanakya uses this method while working out international policies. You may be a strong king in a particular geographical location, but outside your boarders you may be weak. So, when you are in a foreign land or an unknown area, instead of trying to prove your might, find an associate (*mitra*) locally to help you in that new territory. Success is also in accepting that you are not good in everything.

🐎 Right person for the right job

"*Ayogyah purusho nasti, yojakastatra durlabha,*" says *Shukra Niti*. Getting a job is about demand and supply. There is someone looking for work somewhere and somewhere there is work looking for a person to take over. But there are also these rare people who know where the work is and where to find the right people for that. This person is called a *yojaka* — the connector, a rare breed who can bridge the gap between demand and supply.

Chanakya was a mastermind even in the field of economics. He grasped the law of demand and supply. The *Arthashastra's* Book 2 dealing with economic policies is an excellent example of Chanakya's understanding of what needs to be done and where. He was also capable of creating demand and supply as and when required. The whole cycle of demand and supply creates economic activities. This is what made him a great economist.

♞ Everyone is a leader

Leadership qualities are inherent in everyone, only we do not know how to identify it. In most cases it is dormant and you require someone to bring it out. That is the role of a guru. The guru helps to wake that sleeping giant of a leader within each of us. It is like polishing a rough diamond. You need to know that there is a diamond inside you in order for it to shine forth. Give importance to the leadership qualities inside you.

YOU NEED TO KNOW THAT THERE IS A DIAMOND INSIDE YOU IN ORDER FOR IT TO SHINE FORTH. GIVE IMPORTANCE TO THE LEADERSHIP QUALITIES INSIDE YOU.

"One single idea can transform a listless soul into a towering leader among men," said Swami Chinmayananda. Similarly, Chanakya gave a vision to Chandragupta and brought out the leadership qualities in him. The idea in front of Chandragupta was to build a united India. Chanakya not only gave him a dream but also helped him achieve the goal — as a mentor, philosopher and guide. So what is your goal? Who is your mentor? Find the answers and you will soon awaken the leader within you.

♞ Even natural leaders require training

There is a classical question experts keep asking. Are leaders born or made? The answer is quite different. Even if someone is a born leader, he should be trained in the field of leadership. Without adequate preparation, he will not shine going forward. At the same time, everyone is born with certain qualities of leadership. Through training, these qualities can be enhanced and polished. Therefore, getting the right leadership guru is also equally important.

Chanakya was great at identifying leadership talent. After spotting the talent, he would train those students. While Chandragupta was among the most famous of his students, there were many others who became leaders in their own areas of expertise. The *Arthashastra* shows the method to identify leaders (Book 6, Chapter 1, Verse 3) and how to educate them.

♞ Values make a good leader a great leader

There are many good leaders around. What makes good leaders great? It is the values that they hold close to their hearts and principles they follow throughout their life.

Even in the ups and downs of life, if you stick to your principles, the challenges will become easy to handle. Ideals make people and organizations valuable. Therefore, in the leadership space, the worth of a person is the philosophies he follows.

EVEN IN THE UPS AND DOWNS OF LIFE, IF YOU STICK TO YOUR PRINCIPLES, THE CHALLENGES WILL BECOME EASY TO HANDLE. IDEALS MAKE PEOPLE AND ORGANIZATIONS VALUABLE.

Raja dharma defines the duties of a king. However, *dharma* has a much broader meaning than just 'duty'. In the Book 3 of the *Arthashastra* (concerning judges) Chanakya defines *dharma* in various contexts. The word '*dharma*' repeats 150 times in the entire *Arthashastra*. *Dharma* also means values. So, Chanakya was not just a 'Raja Guru' but also a 'Dharma Guru'. He showed to the world that it is the values that stood the test of time.

🐎 Communicate your vision

Your vision is something others cannot see, but it can be shown to them. The leader is the one with the vision. This vision should be crystal clear in the mind of the leader. The next step is to communicate this vision to the followers and other team members. Communicating clearly is an art. The vision statement of an organization is not just something that is written on a piece of paper, but it has to touch the hearts of every person who reads it.

Chanakya stresses on the quality of oratory skills of a leader in Book 6, Chapter 1, Verse 6 of the *Arthashastra*. It is not just about giving speeches and impressing people. According to Chanakya, what your oratory skills speak about is your ability to carry your vision to the hearts and minds of the listeners using just words. Words, when communicated correctly, have the power to invoke confidence among followers. These inspired followers will then translate your vision into reality.

♘ If you want to grow, organize a system

Many people want to grow and be successful but not all of them know how to go about it. It is all right to start alone. Being a 'one man army' is good at the beginning. But as you progress, you will require more and more people to lend you a hand to reach your potential, to achieve your goal. When the team gets bigger and bigger, how do you manage people? For that, you need to put systems and processes in place. All the leaders know that to manage growth, systems have to be put in place. Well-designed systems help you grow and expand.

Chanakya made Chanadragupta Maurya the king of Magadha. But the next level for growth was to come from conquering the whole of Bharat. So how did he do it? Even though there is a king in Magadha, with more kingdoms added to their bounty, Chanakya needed a system to govern all these kingdoms together. So he devised a structure to manage the growth of Chandragupta's new empire and kept the expansion spreading without a glitch.

♞ Organize your mind, organize your work

The Bhagavad Gita is an important part of Indian culture. The discourse of Lord Kṛṣṇa in the midst of the battle field is a guide not only to Arjuna but to each one of us. Even after over five thousand years, the message of the Gita is very relevant. Arjuna, the best warrior among the Pandavas, had lost his ability to think clearly after noticing that he would be fighting half of his family in the Great War. Krishna, with his rousing speech, changed Arjuna's perception about the war and his role in it. It is all in the mind and therefore, one needs to control the mind first.

It is clear that a good mindset is to be developed to make your work productive and effective. A calm state of mind is essential to get the required results. A great leader is the one with a clear head. Chanakya asserted his belief in a productive mind with his concept *aanvikshiki*, the science of inquiry.

♞ Seek help

Once a man was driving and he lost his way. He continued directionless even after a considerable amount of time. Noticing this, one of the fellow passengers asked him, "Why don't you stop and ask for direction?" The driver replied, "Madam, I don't ask anyone for help. I will find the place myself." Now, this kind of thinking is useless. It will only waste time and lead to more confusion. Therefore, when in trouble, stop and ask for help.

A leader may not always know how to act in certain difficult situations. If you ever find yourself in one, keep your ego aside and admit to yourself that you are only human and you need help. According to Chanakya, if a king were to seek help, the council of ministers (*amatya*) should be his first point of contact. Even then if he does not get clarity, he should ask for the help of other experts (*vriddha sanyogah*). Seek help and move forward.

♞ Maintain your dignity, not your ego

There is a thin line between dignity and ego. Ego is dangerous as it can destroy you. Dignity is knowing what you stand for and it will help you to grow. Leaders must have dignity and not ego. Humility is also an essential quality for any great leader. But taking a humble leader for granted is not right. Many people do take leaders for granted but a good leader will show his influence when the need arises. This is the display of dignity at the right place, at the right time.

"*If the rod is not used at all, the stronger swallows the weak in the absence of the wielder of the rod,*" says the *Arthashastra*,

Book 1, Chapter 4, Verses 13-14. He believed that using a rod (any means of reprimand) will frighten people off; it will terrorize people. Also, such leaders may misuse their power to satisfy their ego. But not being strict is something that can make people take their leader for granted. In such situations, to maintain your dignity and respect, be firm in your dealings.

LEADERS MUST HAVE DIGNITY AND NOT EGO. HUMILITY IS ALSO AN ESSENTIAL QUALITY FOR ANY GREAT LEADER. BUT TAKING A HUMBLE LEADER FOR GRANTED IS NOT RIGHT.

🐎 Balance both discipline and love

The presence of both the father and mother is important for the healthy development of the child. Traditionally, the mother is the embodiment of love while the father is the disciplinarian in the family. In the same way, in any country, organization or institute, both love and discipline have to be balanced and maintained for progressive growth.

Chanakya, in his *Arthashastra*, shows us the way to do just that. He is known to be strict and tough, but on the other hand, he was also loving and caring. According to him, the old and the sick in the society have to be taken care of and not to be put to work. *"Old and sick persons should be helped,"* says Verse 28, Chapter 3, Book 5 of the *Arthashastra*. Also, he says that those who are fit and fine have to create wealth for others who are not able to. Thus, he shows that a balance of love and discipline is possible.

♞ Give the young a chance

The youth have energy and enthusiasm while the old have wisdom and experience. Usually, the old do not like to handover their power to the next in line. They cling on to their roles. But only when the youth are empowered to take up leadership roles can the society prosper. However, the old should be around to impart their wisdom and experience to the next generation. Give the youngsters a chance and help them flourish as leaders of a new world.

Chanakya was a wise man and had a lot of experience in political science and governance of a kingdom. However, he did not become king himself. He gave his able student Chandragupta Maurya a chance to rule the kingdom. Therefore, he is known as a kingmaker and not king. Many of us do not trust the young because we believe that they will make mistakes. Everyone learns through mistakes. To speed up their learning process, give them opportunities as early as possible and watch them flourish.

♞ Ordinary can make you extraordinary

Chanakya was an ordinary teacher according to many. But this ordinary person made everyone who listened to his advice extraordinary. That is the power of a great mentor. If you look at history, you will notice many seemingly ordinary human beings who have created legends through trainings and expert guidance. For example, Socrates was an ordinary

The old should impart wisdom to the next generation and help them flourish.

person yet he made his students like Plato think differently and shaped them into brilliant philosophers.

The ability to think creatively makes a person different from the others. Chanakya trained his students in this method of productive thinking — *aanvikshiki*. Your life is shaped by your thoughts. So, be careful from whom you gather your thoughts. Many sages and saints have also transformed their devotees from ordinary to extraordinary beings by imparting useful life lessons to those who have lost all hope.

♞ Trust God completely, but do not trust people blindly

We are often hurt by others, thanks to expectations. Bitter past experiences make us cautious about trusting others further. But this approach is not helpful. Just because someone has hurt you in the past does not mean that you should not trust others. If you had had a partnership that broke up, it does not mean that the future partnerships will also fail. Learn from the past but do not bind your future to it.

> JUST BECAUSE SOMEONE HAS HURT YOU IN THE PAST DOES NOT MEAN THAT YOU SHOULD NOT TRUST OTHERS. LEARN FROM THE PAST BUT DO NOT BIND YOUR FUTURE TO IT.

What to do then? Do not trust people blindly. For example, if you are selecting a new employee for a crucial position in your team, before you bestow your trust upon the person, closely study him for some time. It was Chanakya's method, too, before he took in his key people. He would investigate their background, check their behaviour patterns and only then would he proceed to include them in his fold. The chapter on appointment of ministers in Book 1 of the *Arthashastra* is all about carefully choosing trustworthy people. But always remember that with human beings there could be lack of trust unlike with God. Trust Him completely.

♞ Respect everyone, even your adversary

Someone becomes your enemy because of something you do not like about him. However, there could be some quality even in that person that is worth admiring. But this does not mean that your enemy will become your friend overnight. Instead, this will make you smarter than your rival. In the movie *The Godfather*, there is an interesting dialogue, which goes, "Never hate your enemies. It affects your judgement."

Chanakya used to respect everyone, including his enemies. He believed that there is something in everyone worth learning from. There are many ways of showing admiration to your competitor. One of the methods is diplomacy. Before any war, there are peace talks with the warring nations; the envoys of the countries meet and try to resolve the issues with mutual reverence. With a bit of respect, unnecessary expenditure and mayhem can always be avoided.

♞ War is not just about winning

After a victory, most of us feel a bit arrogant. Chanakya would not have approved of that kind of attitude. Because winning is not the only output required, especially in a battle. Peace for everyone should be the ultimate result of a war. In the *Arthashastra*, Book 15, Chapter 5, Pacification of the Conquered Territory, you will find various situations where after defeating the foe, at times the kingdom is handed back to him.

Similarly, in the *Ramayana*, Rama defeats Ravana and yet he did not take over his enemy's kingdom. Rama rescues his wife Sita, who had been in Ravana's captivity, and then leaves the whole kingdom to Vibhishana, Ravana's brother. He could have easily taken over Lanka, which was richer than Ayodhaya, his own kingdom. But Rama knew his battle was not about land. He fought Ravana to free Sita. Once he achieved his goal, he left everything else in the hands of the rightful owners.

♞ Think both local and global

Globalization is the "it" word today. From the local *kirana* store owner to a CEO of a company, everybody is talking about going global with their products and services. As we become more and more global, we need to understand that globalization is good, but retaining our local roots is equally important. The right approach is to think both local and global. In reality, both are connected to each other. For instance, if you are in some local business, it makes sense to understand the global trends so that your business can benefit from it. On the other hand, it will also help global businesses to study the local market so that they can customize their products and services accordingly.

In the *Arthashastra*, Chanakya provides the right balance between local and global. In Book 7, Chanakya gives both international policies and international relations primary focus. This kind of approach helps build a larger perspective. Even though Chanakya was working within the borders of India, he was always clued-in about what was happening across the globe. He had his eyes and ears glued to the whole world. This quality made Chanakya a formidable thought leader of his generation.

♞ The link between past and future

The future is built on the foundation of the past. Between the past and the future is your present, where you can decide to create the future you wish for. There is a strong link between our past, present and future. Leaders should understand this link because this connection brings in not only the wisdom of the past but also encourages creativity in the future.

Chanakya, in the *Arthashastra*, uses this link between the past and the future to create the present. He used to draw his insight from the wisdom of the ancestors. However, getting stuck in the past is very dangerous. Humanity has progressed much ahead of our forefathers, but those lessons are our guiding light into the future.

🐴 Cultivate both worldly and spiritual thoughts

We live simultaneously in two worlds. The world that is seen, felt and experienced: we call it the physical world. We are connected with the spiritual world, too.

Chanakya used to invoke the gods and deities for success in all his endeavours. In the *Arthashastra*, the king is also advised in his daily rituals to pray to gods and nature. American Businessman and author Stephen Covey said, "We are not human beings on a spiritual journey. We are spiritual beings on a human journey."

🐴 High living, simple thinking

The concept of simple living and high thinking is quite popular. Even though this is true, Chanakya looked at it from another angle — high living and simple thinking. A king is surrounded by wealth and richness. Yet, he should not get carried away by material possessions. Chanakya introduces the term 'Rajarishi' in the *Arthashastra*, a king who is as unassuming as a *rishi* (sage).

ONE SHOULD BE NEUTRAL TO POVERTY AND RICHNESS BECAUSE TIME AND TIDE COULD CHANGE ANY TIME. THERE ARE RAGS TO RICHES STORIES AND RICHES TO RAGS STORIES, TOO.

One should be neutral to poverty and richness because time and tide could change any time. There are rags to riches stories and riches to rags stories, too. India has seen poverty for quite a few generations as invaders and rulers looted us. But even in those times, Indians found happiness in simple living. But now the tide has turned. We are getting back to becoming a developed and rich country again. In the days to come, we too should be able to enjoy wealth. However, always remember to remain detached from the outcome.

Fly with your ideas, but be grounded in reality

Chanakya was a visionary. However, his ideas were not understood by many during his time. The very thought of building a nation from 16 regional kingdoms who were constantly fighting each other seemed impossible. But, Chanakya made it possible. How did he do that? By keeping himself grounded in the realities around. The gap between your vision and reality is hard work.

When life gives you problems, it may seem like you will never be able to solve them. But if you think strategically, you will surely find a solution. You need to keep a cool head in the most trying circumstances. You may need to face some harsh realities, but do not get stuck with them. Keep your vision in your mind and slowly work towards the solution, and you will see the magic unraveling before your eyes. What seemed impossible will become possible. Your vision will be converted into reality.

♞ Chronicle your experiences

"I do not know how to write." This is the first reaction whenever someone is told to pen his thoughts. But that is just a hitch at the beginning. Just take the first step and slowly you will start moving towards your goal. You may not know how to write a book, but it is important that you record your journey. Your book is not just a few words on paper, it is your thoughts presented in words. Your life experiences can guide others, too. You never know when and where you will be inspiring someone.

Imagine if Chanakya had not written *Kautilya's Arthashastra*. He would still have been a great man, but his thoughts and teachings would have been lost. All his wisdom would have been lost after his death. Even today, 2400 years after Chanakya's death, his book continues to inspire many; generations have benefitted from his views. When someone writes a book, he gifts his knowledge and experiences to others. Would Chanakya have ever thought that one day you would be holding this book and you will be gaining from his wisdom?

♞ Talk to advisors, listen to everyone

Listening is a great skill and an art. Most people think listening is equal to hearing and that is not correct. When you listen, you are putting your mind and heart into it. There is full involvement in the process. When you truly listen to anyone, your outlook will change, you gain more wisdom. Therefore, we need to listen to everyone, with full attention. The ability to listen to anyone with 100 percent attention makes a great leader.

We should only talk about our problems and concerns with a few people. It is only natural for leaders to feel lonely at times. But it is important to discuss some of the issues that concern them with someone they trust. So, whom should the leaders talk to and discuss their problems with? According to Chanakya, leaders should seek counsel from their advisors and other wise people in their group (The *Arthashastra*, Book 1, Chapter 15, The Topic of Counsel). This chapter is a guideline on how to seek advice and get an action plan in place to solve our problems.

♞ Do not create confusion, communicate clearly

There is a management technique called 'Management by Confusion'. Sounds funny, but this has been applied by many people. And interestingly, it works. During times of chaos, people tend to run helter-skelter without any direction. And there are some who think that just running itself is work. They think that productivity is based on how much one person can run. For them, the speed and the distance are all that matters. But they will finally realize that they ran a great distance at good speed but ended up in a completely wrong place.

True leadership, according to Chanakya, is not about confusing your people, but giving them direction and clarity. To give clear instructions to someone, one has to learn to communicate well. Both verbal and written communication has to be defined and expressed properly. On the topic of edicts in the *Arthashastra*, Chanakya gives prime importance to written communication. When there is a well-defined system, people work with direction and they reach their goals faster.

♞ Leave your mark

The universe is a strange phenomenon. It existed before us and will be here after us, too. But some people leave their mark on the world. Your life should be such that people remember you even after you are dead and gone. People should remember you for the work you did, the ideals you lived for and the thoughts you left behind.

Chanakya left his mark on the universe. Not only Indian history but world history is not complete without the mention of Chanakya (or Kautilya, his alias). His ideas still has a great impact on our ethos. Our society's value system is created by great men of repute and Chanakya is one among them. If you want to understand the Indian psyche, understand Chanakya first. A study of his life will leave a mark on your life, forever.

♞ Exit gracefully before you are asked to leave

In life, everyone has a part to perform. However, once the part is done, do not hang around. This is true for everyone at every stage of life, especially for the old people. They should be able to retire gracefully. When the young team members are trained and ready, the older ones should be able to walk away, leaving the path for others. The tragedy of life is that no one wants to exit. If you stick around even after your portion is over, others will force you to walk out. It is best to exit gracefully before others come up with an exit plan for you.

THE TRAGEDY OF LIFE IS THAT NO ONE WANTS TO EXIT. IF YOU STICK AROUND EVEN AFTER YOUR PORTION IS OVER, OTHERS WILL FORCE YOU TO WALK OUT.

Chanakya, when his job was done, gracefully walked out of the king's court. When Chandragupta's son Bindusara became the king, Chanakya retreated to the forest to teach the next generation of students. No one wanted him to leave the court, but Chanakya knew that there is a limit to oneself. His work was done as a king's mentor and he left it to others to carry forward his good efforts. When such clarity of thinking dawns on us, we become wise.

Simplicity should not be taken for granted

There was a snake who once heard a saint asking people to never hurt anyone. The snake was touched by the words of the great man and stopped biting people. This created a rumour that the snake had lost its power to bite. People started throwing stones at it and finally it almost came face to face with death. One day, the saint was passing by the injured snake. When he enquired about what happened, the snake told the story. The saint realized what a fool the snake had been. He said, "I told you not to hurt anyone, never did I tell you to stop hissing at people." That could have protected the snake from people's attack.

Life is strange. Those who are humble are taken for granted while those who are boisterous and make noise are taken seriously. Chanakya knew when to remain calm and when to make his presence felt. He was a simple man, but nobody could take him for granted. He was insulted for his simplicity at the court of King Dhanananda. But when the time came, he challenged Dhanananda and defeated him. His life is a powerful message: never take an unassuming person for granted.

♞ If you do not stand up for something, you will fall for everything

While addressing a group of youngsters, Swami Tejomayananda, a senior monk from the Chinmaya Mission, said, "When you plan your life, have long-term, medium-term and short-term goals." The idea was to give them a roadmap of life. He continued by saying, "Also remember, if you do not stand up for something, you will fall for everything." We all should have an ideal in life. That ideal will keep us inspired and going when challenges block our way.

How did Chanakya live his life? He had an ideal for which he stood up — it was 'Bharat', a united India. The concept of *rashtra nirman*, nation building, kept him going. He was all alone when he started on his journey. He met with various challenges along the way. But when you keep your eyes glued to your goal, every problem becomes easy to handle. Without a goal, even in the best of circumstances you will feel lazy to march on.

♞ Study philosophy and psychology

If you study the *Arthashastra* and the life of Chanakya, two things are difficult to miss. Chanakya was a philosopher and a master psychologist. The *Arthashastra* starts with 'the establishment of philosophy'. He used to make sure that future leaders are given training in philosophical thinking. Next is the study of the human mind. People are different and dealing with different types of people is an art. For that, one needs to study psychology.

Even in the field of modern management, both the subjects of philosophy and psychology are given a lot of importance. The philosophy of management has become a very important subject of research. Today's popular discussion topics like industrial psychology, consumer behaviour, etc., are subjects that have roots in psychology. Philosophy makes you a master of yourself while psychology makes you a master of others.

THE PHILOSOPHY OF MANAGEMENT HAS BECOME A VERY IMPORTANT SUBJECT OF RESEARCH. PHILOSOPHY MAKES YOU A MASTER OF YOURSELF WHILE PSYCHOLOGY MAKES YOU A MASTER OF OTHERS.

♞ Everyone understands economics

Economics is a highly respected field of study. An economist is an expert who studies the relationship between a nation/society's resources and its production/output. Research findings and opinions of economists are used in shaping policies such as tax laws, interest rates, employment programmes, trade agreements, etc. Countries have senior positions like chief economic advisor to the prime minister while large corporations employ a chief economist to understand the market. The role of an economist cannot be underestimated. Think like an economist, they know much more than others.

Chanakya is considered the Father of Indian Economics. He, too, had a deep understanding of financial models and subjects related to wealth creation. But it is not right to say that only the intellectuals understand economics. Even a common man will understand some aspect of economics. Whenever we deal with money on a daily basis, we are in effect thinking like economists. Therefore, everyone can understand economics if it is explained in simple, day-to-day terms, and everyone should strive to understand the subject a little more.

♞ Teach your children to think

A Chinese saying goes this way: "Never limit your children to your thoughts because they are born in a different era." There is a tendency among parents to make their children think like themselves. While it is important for the parents to pass on their life experiences to their children, never limit them with your experiences. Because with every generation time changes and with changing times how we think also changes. Therefore, train your children to have original minds.

In the famous *Chanakya Niti Sutra*, Chanakya says, "Till five years love your children, for the next ten years discipline them, after that consider them your friends." So, once your children are above 15 years of age, consider them your equals. Learn how to think differently from your children.

♞ Give teachers freedom

Teachers are a very important part of any society. The future of a nation depends on its education system. Education decides the way the next generation grows up. Unfortunately in India we have created an examination system rather than an education system. Every parent is worried about their children's marks and there is heavy competition everywhere. Education has become a rat race. But this was not so in the past; our ancient gurukul education system was different. The core of this system was personality development and improvement of character of the students.

Chanakya, the great teacher, also designed the education system for his generation. In the *Arthashastra*, Book 1, Chapter 1, he details the syllabus to be taught to the students. Teachers were given the freedom to design the program as they wanted. They were also given the freedom to test the students using their own methods. When teachers are given liberty, the best within them comes out. Only the best students will come out of such an education system.

♞ Teaching is not just a job but a great responsibility

While teachers should be given the freedom to choose their teaching methods, it is also important that the teachers understand their responsibilities. Unfortunately, for most teachers of our generation, teaching has become just another profession. While teaching should provide money and livelihood, a teacher is not just another worker. Teaching is the premier profession that shapes all other professions.

Chanakya was just another teacher in the lot. He became extraordinary because he was self-motivated and inspired to make a change. He said, "Teachers are not ordinary; creation and destruction both play in their laps." (From *Chanakya*, the TV series by Dr. Chandraprakash Dwivedi.) Teaching is a great responsibility because teachers shape the next generation.

♞ Anyone can be a leader

Yes, anyone can be a leader. It is a myth that only the top brass are leaders. However, the truth is that there is a leader in each one of us. Even your office boy is a leader in his own capacity. But he may not know his own potential. Therefore, the best thing to do is to allow everyone's leadership qualities to come out. If you are a leader, create an eco-system in your organization where each of your subordinates starts making decisions.

THERE IS A LEADER IN EACH ONE OF US. IF YOU ARE ALREADY A LEADER, CREATE AN ECO-SYSTEM IN YOUR ORGANIZATION WHERE EACH OF YOUR SUBORDINATES STARTS MAKING DECISIONS.

Chanakya had created many leaders — some big, some small. Even though the most popular one was Chandragupta, his other students, too, went on to become leaders in their own chosen professions. As a scholar once said, "The knowledge of the *Arthashastra* helps a small kingdom to protect itself from larger kingdoms, and also for a big kingdom to remain big." So the size of the kingdom/organization/project does not matter, what matters is leadership qualities that each of us have within us.

♞ Anyone can be a teacher

In India, teaching remains the most respected profession even today. Now, one does not have to necessarily work at any prestigious educational institution to become a teacher. Even if you are tutoring a single student, you are still a teacher and have the

TRAINING AND DISCIPLINE ARE ACQUIRED BY ACCEPTING THE AUTHORITATIVENESS OF THE TEACHERS IN THE RESPECTIVE FIELDS.

potential to become a great one at that. Samarth Ramadas was a personal mentor and guide to King Shivaji while Chanakya taught thousands of students. So, learn from every educator you come across and try to be a tutor yourself.

Whatever little we know, if we can transfer that knowledge and experience to others, we automatically become teachers. Share and spread your knowledge. *"Training and discipline are acquired by accepting the authoritativeness of the teachers in the respective fields."* — The *Arthashastra*, Book1, Chapter 5, Verse 6.

♞ Gather wisdom from everywhere

Many complain of boredom. We get bored because our mind reaches a point of non-learning. If we are continuously observing and learning from others, we will never get bored. So learn to gather wisdom from everywhere possible. When the mind develops a flair for continuous observation, we start getting insights, the inherent wisdom of our subconscious. Chanakya wanted his students to develop a mind capable of insights and intuitions.

Even when we are alone, we can gather wisdom from inside us. Chanakya's suggestion of daily pondering will help us to develop analytical skills. Also a keen sense of observations gets developed in the process. In the *Arthashatra*, he also touches the point of a king mastering yoga. Yoga helps to calm the mind, providing clarity to one's thoughts.

♞ See what is not visible

All that glitters is not gold. The human mind is trained to see the external appearances as it is. So it is easier to be fooled by what is in front of our eyes. However, those who are smart go beyond what is in front of them. Try to see what is not shown to you. Do not judge the book by its cover. Inside the pages there could be something totally beyond your imagination. Think twice before you come to a conclusion on anything that is present to you, be it information, choices, facts, anything. Think beyond what is obvious.

Chanakya trained his students to think outside everything that is seen and shown. How does one do that? Look at things critically, ask questions, be curious. Chanakya used to even check the quality of gold presented to the king to make sure of the quality. A palace has many secret passages known only to a few trusted insiders. If you are smart, inspecting the wall carefully, you will be able to locate the obscure room behind it that will lead to the passage. Be that person who tries to find that secret passage in every situation.

♘ Listen to what is not said

When people speak, they only convey just a fraction of what is actually going on inside their minds. There is almost always a difference between what one thinks and says in public. The person who can understand this becomes good at reading people. Develop a quality of listening to unspoken words — facial expressions, gestures, tone of voice, eye contact, pauses, etc. You will be able to gather more information about the person and what he is trying to say this way.

Chanakya taught his students to think while listening to others. In the *Arthashastra*, he talks about studying the background of a person one is having a conversation with; this will lead to understanding the nuances of what the person is talking about. As you begin to get to know people, you will also realize that most of the times individuals really do not mean what they say.

♞ Read between the lines

Like understanding the words not spoken, reading between the lines (sometimes quite literally), is critical in having a successful communication. Books have always been the keepers of history. However, merely devouring printed words without giving them a second thought is as good as not reading at all. Try to understand the intent and the spirit of the words as you go through the pages. Sometimes you may have to read a book a couple of times to fully grasp the idea the author is trying to convey.

In the *Arthashastra*, Chanakya puts a lot of emphasis on well-documented government records. But what is more important is that he also trains his students to read the past records. A prince has to read the records of the former hundred years of the kingdom as a part of his education. Through this activity, the prince will come to know about the challenges faced in the past and how his ancestors resolved them. Thus, with insights from the past, he can become a good king in the future.

♞ *Aanvikshiki* is the ultimate knowledge

Knowledge can be acquired through educational institutions, through life experiences, through learning about men of wisdom and their works, etc. But the best way to attain awareness is through one's own thinking; Chanakya called this method 'Aanvikshiki' — the science of strategic thinking.

According to Chanakya, *Aanvikshiki* is the first and the most important method to attain wisdom for a king. It is called *prathama vidya* in the *Arthashastra*, Book 1 Also, it is the ultimate knowledge. He wanted his students to think, question, apply logic and then come to their own conclusions about a topic. This eliminates the herd mentality. So if you want to succeed in life, practice *aanvikshiki*.

Be on the right side of the law

A good citizen of any nation will abide by the laws of the nation. Those who break the law become criminals and are punished according to the constitution. In the same way, one needs to be on the right side of the cosmic law or dharma as well. If we do not follow the path of dharma, we are practicing adharma — illegal or immoral actions — in the eyes of the universe. It is always the people on the right side of the law who turn out to be the winners at the end.

IF WE DO NOT FOLLOW THE PATH OF DHARMA, WE ARE PRACTICING ADHARMA — ILLEGAL OR IMMORAL ACTIONS — IN THE EYES OF THE UNIVERSE.

In Book 3 of the *Arthashastra* called Dharmasthiya, Chanakya lays down rules for the citizens as well as the king. Even the king or the leader has to follow the law. If the leader misuses or breaks the law, he should be punished. In fact, according to Chanakya, if a common man is punished for a crime, the government employee who has committed the same crime must be punished twice and the king, for the same crime, should be given the same punishment four times, because they hold higher stakes. Therefore, a leader has to be a keeper of the law himself.

♞ Be just

Leadership is about responsibility. Since it comes with certain powers, the chance to misuse these powers is also high. This is why before becoming a leader it is important for the chosen person to be trained in handling power. In traditions across the world you will notice that a leader, king, queen, is depicted with a rod in hand. This rod is symbolism for punishing the wicked and protecting the innocent. So, be just while using your power as a leader.

The *Arthashastra* says that a king impartial with the rod is respected and honoured by his people. If not, he is either feared for using the rod too much or taken for granted for not using it at all. A good leader has to understand justice in order to be just.

♞ Clear thinking leads to right decisions

The ability to analyze and think through various angles and possibilities leads to good decisions. Those who are trained in critical thinking also look at the impact of their verdicts; the outcomes, both short term and long term, have to be considered carefully. Therefore, all good choices are a result of strategic thinking and logical conclusions.

It is also crucial to take decisions fast during a crisis situation. You may not have too much time to think during such times; yet you have to consider all the pros and cons of your choices. In the *Arthashastra*, in the chapters dealing with the art of war (Books 9-14), Chanakya discusses decision making as a quality to be developed by a leader. As a leader, your one decision can affect many people and their lives, therefore, it is important to learn how to take the right decisions at the right time with clarity of thought.

♞ Understand your duty before you do your duty

Most people go through life without any direction. If you randomly tell someone to run, that person may start running impulsively, such is people's disconnect with their own selves. They will not even ask you why. Similarly, in life we should understand our duty before we start doing our part so that we can fulfil it better.

IN AN ORGANIZATION, IF YOU ARE NOT AWARE OF WHAT IS EXPECTED OF YOU, PLEASE ASK SOMEONE OF AUTHORITY AND GET CLARITY ABOUT YOUR ROLE BEFORE YOU START WORK.

Under Chanakya's tutelage, a king is taught his duty or *raja dharma* before he is crowned (The *Arthashastra*, Book 1, Chapter 19, Rules for the King). In the similar manner, the other officers of the kingdom — the ministers, the commander of the army, other government officials — all of them were clearly instructed about their responsibilities beforehand. In an organization, if you are not aware of what is expected of you, please ask someone of authority and get clarity about your role before you start work.

♞ Study every day

Buddha was on his death bed. His disciples from across the globe came to see their master for one last time. He spent time with each of them. A disciple asked him, "Are you teaching each of them something?" Buddha said, "No, I am learning from each of them, a new lesson before I die." This is the attitude of great masters; they are students forever.

Even after completing their studies at *gurukul*, Chanakya wanted his students to keep learning on a daily basis. For example, a king was supposed to do *swadhyaya* (study on his own) every day. This was essential to keep the mind alert and receptive to any change or new development. Most of the times we take our educational qualifications as the only knowledge required. However, world is changing daily and new information is being generated tirelessly. To keep pace with this growth, acquire knowledge till your last breath.

♞ Give with joy but think before you give

Giving without expecting anything in return is the form of true love. It is only through such an act that we rise above our little self. There is a wonderful saying in India: "Gather with hundred hands and give away with a thousand." Everyone should earn well and then give it back to the society many times more. This is how a society becomes prosperous. Only by giving back does wealth get circulated among others and lead to happiness.

One should donate with joy, without any misgivings. However, think before you do so. How much you give and to whom are also important. Do not throw away your money impulsively. Are you helping the needy? Is the money going to those deserving? How much is enough? Think about these questions before you open your wallet, so that you do not regret later. Also, do not ponder over these questions forever; you may stop contributing altogether.

♞ Create wealth, for yourself and others

Wealth is never an individual entity. It is always collective. Those who understand the principles of wealth creation know that prosperity is interdependent. If there is someone earning money, it is because there are many who are involved in creating it. Wealth comes from the society and it has to go back to the society as well. So earn wealth not only for yourself but for also others — for your family, your employees, for the country and the world.

The *Arthashastra* is about understanding the flow of wealth. Chanakya was a brilliant economist who cracked the code of wealth creation. When someone sets out to be a winner, he has to take others along, too. Richness has to be shared and distributed. A selfish person will never understand the secret to getting rich.

♞ Take another birth in this birth

In India, many believe in rebirth. According to Hindu scriptures, the ultimate aim for a human being is *moksha* or freedom from rebirths. Till we achieve that, we will have to keep taking births one after the other and pay off our karmic debts. But the concept of birth is not just about being born from the mother's womb; one can be reborn after acquiring wisdom. So, we human beings have the ability to take two births in the same life. Those who are reborn through knowledge are known as *dwija* or the twice-born.

HISTORY WOULD NOT HAVE REMEMBERED CHANDRAGUPTA IF HE HAD NOT BECOME A STUDENT OF CHANAKYA, HAD HE NOT TAKEN A SECOND BIRTH AS HIS DISCIPLE.

Chanakya knew when he took in Chandragupta Maurya, an ordinary village urchin, to train him to be a king, that he was giving him a second birth. Such a chance at a rebirth is indeed rare. With the knowledge imparted by Chanakya, Chandragupta became an ideal king. History would not have remembered Chandragupta if he had not become a student of Chanakya, had he not taken a second birth as his disciple.

♞ Know what to do and what not to do

The famous Serenity Prayer says, "God, grant me the serenity to accept the things I cannot change, courage to change the things I can, and the wisdom to know the difference." Therefore, as we work towards our goals, we need to know the difference between what to do and what not to do. Wisdom lies in working hard towards your goal, but leaving the results to God. No, this does not make one lazy. In fact, it is a sign of maturity to do the best and let go the rest.

Many ask, "Could not Chanakya himself have become the king, instead of making Chandragutpa, his student, sit on the throne?" Yes, he could have easily become the king. But he was wise and knew that he was good at teaching and that was the role he loved the most. Why become a king when you can be a kingmaker? A kingmaker is always higher in stature than the king, and therefore, Chanakya preferred to be a teacher all his life.

♞ Worship

Worshipping God is a helpful practice because resolute faith in Him helps us sail through the difficulties in life smoothly. If you start out your day offering obeisance to the almighty, that feeling of divinity stays with you all through the day. You can climb any mountain if you have faith.

Chanakya worshipped gods as well as men of wisdom. He opens *Kautilya's Arthashastra* by paying his respects to Brihaspati and Shukra — *"Om namah Shukra Brihaspati abhyam."* Both were great warriors and teachers, Shukra to Asuras (demons) and Brihaspati to Devas (gods). He also gave due respect to others who served the society in their respective professions. Finally the result is the same: by honouring others, you reach the state of perfection.

♞ Always be active

We do not have a choice but to work. The moment we are born till we die, we have to keep working. "But when I am sleeping, I am not working, right?" one may wonder. Even when you are asleep, your internal organs are toiling away to keep you alive. The moment they stop, you are dead. The *Arthashastra* says, –*"Rajyo hi vratam uttanam* (Book 1, Chapter 19)." To be ever active is the oath of a king.

Swami Chinmayananda once said, "If I rest, I rust." You may take a break in between, but it must be in order to rejuvenate yourself so that you can perform even better.

A lazy man is a liability and burden to all others around. An unproductive person is not liked by anyone. Therefore, just get up and show up. One must have a goal in mind to keep him energized throughout his life. What is the use of health if you are not going to put it to good use? A man with a purpose will continue to work even when he is unwell.

⚘ Help others but do not do their work for them

Being helpful is a good virtue. However, do not be a junkyard where others dump their responsibilities. Lending a hand is all right as long as it does not turn the other person lazy; he should not expect you to do his job. Always remember that you are a human being and you also have your limits. Do not get bogged down by other people's workload. Be helpful and not a slave to others.

ALWAYS REMEMBER THAT YOU ARE HUMAN AND YOU ALSO HAVE YOUR LIMITS. DO NOT GET BOGGED DOWN BY OTHER PEOPLE'S WORKLOAD. BE HELPFUL AND NOT A SLAVE TO OTHERS.

Chanakya lists out the role of a king at length in the *Arthashastra*. The king should be supported by his ministers but a king must not do a minister's work. He can help them with resources and delegate them work. Swapping roles can confuse people and can lead to chaos in the kingdom/ organization.

🐎 A wise man knows his duty

In the Indian culture, duty or dharma is a very important word. It defines your very attitude towards life. One goes through various stages and responsibilities in life. We start out in life as students, we grow to have families and once our children are old enough to handle their responsibilities, we retire from active life. A wise person knows his duty at every stage of life and goes through all the stages with dignity.

The *Arthashastra* lays down the roles and duties of citizens based on the *varna* or the caste system of the Vedic times. As for the leader, when his duties are done, he should retire and give up all the power bestowed upon him. When you give up willingly, you rise up in life.

🐎 Mix with others but do not get carried away

Humans are social animals. And at the same time we are also individuals. It is important to find a balance between being a part of the society and maintaining our individuality. Therefore, we need to learn the art of mixing with others but not getting swayed by their influence. Cultivate your own personality. Have your own opinions and viewpoints; at the same time respect others' thoughts, too.

To achieve this fine balance, Chanakya suggests spending quality time both with other people as well as alone. Do not be selfish but do not forget your 'self'. Mingling with others broadens one's perspective; however, try to have your own views on any matter.

Financial success is important to get ahead in life

Our understanding of money has to be crystal clear to succeed in life. For a businessman, financial success equals to business success. There is no doubt that if you do not pay your employees on time you will not be called a successful businessman. Similarly, if you do not succeed financially, you will not be considered a success in society; a pitiful way of assessing one's growth, but it is the truth. This does not mean that one should run after money alone. However, do not neglect the power of wealth; with wealth at your disposal, you can do much good in life.

IF YOU DO NOT SUCCEED FINANCIALLY, YOU WILL NOT BE CONSIDERED A SUCCESS IN SOCIETY; A PITIFUL WAY OF ASSESSING ONE'S GROWTH, BUT IT IS THE TRUTH.

According to Chanakya, "*Arthaeva pradhanah*" — wealth is important. He believed that for a kingdom to succeed, it needed to have a good economic structure. Also for a king to be called a successful king, he needs to make his citizens rich. This external material richness is very important along with inner spiritual richness. It is the bitter reality of life that only those individuals who have achieved some level of financial success in their lives are given importance in the world.

♞ Security leads to progress

The first and most essential requirement for a person is security — whether we are talking about physical, financial or national security. To begin with, one has to be sure that there is no threat to life. If a person is living in constant fear of being attacked and losing his life, then he can make no progress. If people do not flourish, society remains poor. A society thrives only in a safe environment.

Therefore, Chanakya took care of all types of securities in Chandragupta's kingdom — from physical to financial and social security. This ensured that there was progress and development. When the mind is without fear, it can be put to good use. First World nations are prosperous because their people's basic needs have been met.

♞ Get training from the best

A man shifted from one city to another. He was already learning flute in the previous city and now he was looking for a new flute teacher. He located a reputed flautist and turned up at his house. There was a notice regarding the fees at the door and it read, "For new students, the fee is ₹500

A good teacher knows what kind of training is required for his student to shine in the latter's area of interest.

a month. For students with initial training, the fee is ₹5000 a month." Surprised, the student asked the teacher why a trained student is charged more. The teacher said, "I have to put in more effort to undo the previous baggage of lessons before I teach them anything new."

A good teacher knows what kind of training is required for his student to shine in his area of interest. In the *Arthashastra*, Book 1, Chapter 5, Verse 6, Chanakya says, "Get training from the best." So select your guru carefully. For those who know the value of quality will also know the value of expert guidance. The best in the field will only make you better.

Do not ask the right question to the wrong person

Can you ask a history question to a biology teacher and if he does not provide a satisfactory answer, peg him as a bad history teacher? The problem is that most of us seek our answers from the wrong people. Know who you approach before you expect expert guidance.

Chanakya wanted the king to be surrounded by experts, and these specialists were from various fields. He made sure the king's immediate circle had economists, spiritual gurus, law makers, war strategists, etc. Whenever there was a crisis, these professionals were consulted; this way, the king had the resources at hand for solving any issue concerning the smooth running of the kingdom.

♘ Be always in touch with your teachers

THE OLDER A TEACHER GETS, THE WISER HE BECOMES. AND IT IS ALSO THE RESPONSIBILITY OF THE STUDENTS TO SERVE AND TAKE CARE OF THEIR TEACHERS WHEN THEY GET OLD.

Teachers are not just the ones you need to help you get through schools and universities; they are lifelong assets. A good student is the one who is always curious and ready to imbibe new lessons. And great teachers are treasure chests of knowledge; dig deep, and you will always end up with a jewel or another.

Chanakya introduces the concept of *vriddhasanyogah* in the *Arthashastra*, Book 1, Chapter 5. *Vriddhasanyogah* refers to association with elders; the elderly possesses a wealth of experience and any young person can benefit from being close to people who have seen the world more than him. The older a teacher gets, the wiser he becomes. And it is also the responsibility of the students to serve and take care of their teachers when they get old. This is why the bond between Chanakya and Chandragupta was a special one; they took care of each other at appropriate times.

♘ Be smart, but do not act smart

Intelligence is not something that can been seen, unlike a pretty face, a good hairstyle or a stylish outfit. Intelligence is a very subtle part of your personality that can be developed but not necessarily understood by others. Unlike bodybuilding where muscles can be seen growing stronger and fitter, growth of someone's intellect is too fine to be measured.

Chanakya was very bright, but he was also absolutely unassuming. He looked like any ordinary man, but had a razor-sharp mind, which could see through anything in the split of a second. He also developed that acumen through observation and constant learning. Our lives should be also like that, trying constantly to develop our intellect or *aanvikshiki*, as explained in Book 1, Chapter 2 of the *Arthashastra*.

♞ At the peak is the danger of downfall

Suppose you have climbed the Mount Everest, the highest point on earth. Where do you go from there? From here starts the danger; the danger of a fall. From the top, there is no way but down. So when you are at the peak, you have to be very careful about what you do next. Because it is not just about you, it is also about others. When you are an achiever, others look upon you for inspiration.

Chanakya had taken Chandragupta to the pinnacle, by making him 'Samrat', an emperor of united India. There was nothing bigger to achieve after that in India. Now, Chanakya also knew this is the point from where one has to be careful. Ego can slowly creep in. So he suggested Chandragupta to practice *indriyajaya* or self-control (The *Arthashastra*, Book 1, Chapter 6. With his senses safely under his control,

Chanakya envisioned that Chandragupta could be at the peak forever.

♞ Be careful in the company of leaders, they can make or break you

According to Chanakya, kings are like fire. They can give you warmth and protection. But, if you are not careful, you can also get burnt. People in the leadership positions can either be your protective shield or ruin you. So one should be careful in the company of leaders. Dealing with leaders is an art in itself, because most of them have massive egos that are easily bruised as a result of their success.

IF SOMEBODY IS IN THE WRONG MOOD, EVEN IF YOU CONVEY THE RIGHT THING, IT CAN BE MISUNDERSTOOD AND CAN BACKFIRE, ESPECIALLY IF THAT SOMEONE IS YOUR BOSS.

In the corporate world there is a misunderstanding that being in the good books of the boss means always accepting everything the boss says. Being a good subordinate is not about that. The ability to understand your leader and knowing when to speak are what makes you a good follower. Also, as a trustworthy subordinate, it is your duty to alert the boss if anything is amiss, but do it in a pleasant way. Also, success is in the timing. If somebody is in the wrong mood, even if you convey the right thing, it can be misunderstood and can backfire, especially if that someone is your boss.

♞ Reveal your secrets only to the right person, at the right time

Secrets are a part of leadership. There is a saying in Sanskrit, "When two people are speaking something in secret, only four ears should listen." No third person should know what is happening. Chanakya believed that one should scan the surroundings before starting any secret conversation.

This does not mean that we should always be secretive. Reveal the secrets to others when the time is right. However, choose your audience right. Certain secrets have to be shared with respect and should not fall in the wrong ears. That is why in the ancient times *brahma vidya*, a highly spiritual revelation, is shared by the gurus only with the mature and highly-evolved students knows as *adhikaris*, the deserving ones.

♞ Choose your leaders carefully

One man, one vote was the policy adopted by the creators of the Indian constitution when we got freedom from the Raj. Vote is the power given to the common man in a democratic country to choose his leaders. There are still countries where the citizens do not have this power, so use it carefully. Choose your leaders judiciously, because they are in a position to determine not only your future but the future of many generations to come.

Even though there was no voting system during those days,

Chanakya spent a lot of time choosing his leaders. Out of many brilliant students that he had, he only chose one Chandragupta to be the king of Magadha. The reason was that Chandragupta was the closest to the perfect leader that Chanakya has envisioned. Even though Chandragupta had the potential and all the leadership qualities required, he still needed thorough training to shape him as a great leader. Even those who are born with leadership qualities should be trained.

♞ Do not forget the past

Forgive and forget, goes the well-known saying. But that is not how leaders should think; forgive but do not forget. Any mistakes or misgivings should be looked at as lessons and one must learn from them. Many a times, history repeats; your past may come back. Nobody wants to repeat their past mistakes; so learn your valuables lessons from them and make sure you do not repeat them in future. Forgetting is not a wise course of action for those who want to grow in life.

Chanakya spent all his life carefully analyzing the threats to Chandragupta Maurya's empire. When Chandragupta defeated Alexander the Great, Chanakya knew that Alexander may come back. Remember, your adversary will never be happy with his defeat. He will be constantly preparing for his comeback. Even though Alexander died on his way back, Chanakya knew better than to forget the past. He made sure he documented all strategies he used in the war against Alexander in his book, the *Arthashastra*, so that future generations can benefit from it.

♞ Promote capable people

In any organization, there are various types of people — some are capable, some can be trained to do more and some are just incapable. In all these cases, the leader/boss plays a major role. For one, a leader should be able to understand the difference between the various types, because he has to work with others to get the results and complete projects. So assessing the capability of others is a very essential and handy leadership quality.

And those who are capable should be promoted. When the time comes for selecting a leader in an organization, either one can bring in a person from the outside or promote someone within the existing team. Chanakya always gave first preference to those capable persons within the kingdom. Only if he could not find anyone suitable within the ranks did he seek people outside.

♞ Trust only the worthy

Do not bestow your trust on just anyone. However, to be able to truly take someone into confidence is no small feat, because it is about being close to someone and letting them

NO ONE SUCCEEDS
IN LIFE ALONE;
THERE IS ALWAYS
A TEAM THAT
WORKS BEHIND
THE WINNER. IN
ORDER TO GET
AHEAD, YOU NEED
TO TRUST PEOPLE
TO HELP YOU.

in on your true self without having the fear that they will betray you or misuse their closeness to you. To be able to rely on other people in the hour of need and in turn be worthy of other people's should be your aim in life. No one succeeds in life alone; there is always a team that works behind the winner. In order to get ahead, you need to trust people to help you.

Chanakya stresses on the concept of *mitra* (friend or ally) in the *Arthashastra*. According to Book 6, Chapter 1, one of the qualities of a good *mitra* is being trustworthy. In the olden days, a king took only his close allies when he went into a battle; if they were not reliable, they could stab him at the back. Also remember that it is a two-way street, you have to be dependable first for people to return the favour.

♞ Understand emotions but do not become emotional

Human beings have complex emotions, an evolutionary tool bestowed on us to cope with specific situations. Since man is a social animal, emotions also help us connect with others and rely on each other for survival. Man as a species is also highly intelligent, who can take care of his own needs. However, the challenge is to balance emotions and intelligence. Many people find it hard to keep matters of the heart at bay when it comes to making decisions.

Chanakya was one such person who understood human emotions and had a grip over them. He too had feelings but he did not get carried away by them. He applied logic and critical thinking (*aanvikshiki*) instead of feelings while taking decisions. How does one decide whether to use his head or his heart in a situation? This conflict can be solved by asking: what is the purpose? This will give you the clarity and direction required to make up your mind.

🐴 A leader has to be a thinker and a doer

Chanakya wanted active leaders, intelligent and dynamic. But active leaders should also be able to ideate. There are many brilliant thinkers who are unable to execute their ideas, and there are also excellent facilitators who cannot be bothered with thinking and planning. The ideal combination for a leader is that of a thinker and a doer.

When you take up any project, you need to plan the details of how you are going to carry it out properly. Then you need to put together a team that can take the responsibility of the project. Finally through proper supervision you need to ensure that they are finishing the project within the given budget and timeline. One more aspect of good project management is to create a good project report so that in the future anyone can refer to it and learn from it.

♞ Do not break your promise

There is a popular *doha* (couplet) in the *Ramcharitmanas* by poet Tulasidas, *"Raghukul reet sada chali aayi, pran jaye par vachan na jaye"*. It means it is the practice in the dynasty of Raghu (in which Lord Rama was born) to never break a promise, even at the cost of one's life. These were the value systems that our ancestors followed.

One should not go back on a promise. However, Chanakya had a different view altogether on the matter. According to him, it is always better to think twice before you commit to something. The oath taken should not be broken at the cost of life, but the person taking the oath has to be sure of the consequences that may arise in the future. Better think through all the pros and cons before you give your word. It is better to not give someone any hope at all rather than not deliver.

♞ Be open-minded

To be creative and innovative, one has to cultivate a mind devoid of pre-conceived notions and prejudices. It is often a tiny spark that gives birth to groundbreaking discoveries. These sparks can come from anywhere, from within you or from others around you. Look around you, the world is full of inspiration. There is a difference between clarity of mind and rigidity. If you are unyielding about only your views being better, you are killing the spark.

Chanakya was a man of ideas. He even thought of the concept of a 'nation', beyond a kingdom. But even though he was dealing with his own ideas, he did not dismiss the ideas of others. In the *Arthashastra* he says, "A wise man should make use of the sensible words of even a child."

♘ Be firm, not rigid

Being firm is productive. On the other hand, if you are too firm, you become rigid, which is not helpful. One of the interesting things about clear thinking is that it leads to firmness. Being firm is a good quality to have for anyone to be successful. But if you are not clear in your thinking, it can lead to rigidity. For example, in the Ramayana, after Ravan kidnaps Sita and takes her to Lanka, everyone advised him to return Sita to her family. But Ravan's ego made him discard good counsel. Finally, when Ram came with his army to rescue Sita, Ravan not only lost his kingdom but even his life.

Chanakya had a firm personality and was unwavering in his dealing. He had taken an oath to destroy the Nanda dynasty and so he did. Though he was firm and determined to achieve his goals, he was also flexible about the route he took towards the goal. If one way did not work, he was ready to try another. Thus he came up with the four-fold alternatives — *sama, dana, bheda* and *danda*. Keep an open mind about the alternative approaches you need to win the game.

♞ Right time and right timing

There is a big difference between 'right time' and 'right timing'. Even though both seem to be interconnected, there is a fine difference between the two. For example, there is a right time to meet a person, and after meeting that person, deciding when to talk to him is about the right timing. In the olden days, kings met with subjects on a daily basis during an allocated time (right time). But what to speak in front of the king, assessing his mood (right timing) determines the success of your chat.

Throughout the 6000 sutras of the *Arthashastra*, Chanakya gives us tips on when and how to get what you want, be it the routine of a king or the war chapters or how to build strong economic models for a kingdom. A combination of right time and timing leads to success.

♞ It is all about leadership

Bhishma, the great warrior of the epic *Mahabharata*, was a man of wisdom. He was also an expert on *raja niti* or political science. Towards the end of the Mahabharata war, Yudhishtir asked Bhishma a question, "Does an era create a leader or does a leader create an era?" Bhishma replied, "Do not ever doubt this — the king creates an era." Finally, it is all about leadership.

Chanakya was also someone who thought on the same lines — leaders are of utmost importance. Whatever they do, the others will follow. So creating the best leaders is something that he worked on lifelong. The king maker, the strategist, the teacher, the political thinker, the statesman, the visionary, the author of the *Arthashastra*, Chanakya had only one goal — create world-class leaders. Because when you look back at an era, it is about the leaders of that era.

♞ Delegate and monitor work

You can delegate work but you cannot delegate responsibility. Many people do not understand this and then finally when a project fails, they start the blame game. For instance, in an organization, a manager has a team working under him on various projects, most of whom are his juniors. When something goes wrong with a project, the boss cannot blame his juniors or team members and get away with it. The charge of the work not getting done still lies with the leader. Therefore, after delegating work, monitoring it is also a leader's obligation.

Chanakya had made many checks and balances in his system to make sure the responsibility of any initiative rests on the leader's shoulder alone. In the olden days, a king would start various projects and activities but he would then delegate the same to his ministers to carry out. However, if the initiative fails, he cannot blame the ministers. The success or failure of a project depends on the leader's corrective actions from time to time, during the time of the work.

🐎 Do your part and let God do His

TO HAVE THE BLESSINGS OF THE DIVINE, CHANAKYA HAD THE HABIT OF INVOKING VARIOUS DEITIES BEFORE HE STARTED ANYTHING NEW, BE IT A BATTLE OR WRITING A BOOK.

Success is a combination of one's hard work and divine blessing. One without the other will not culminate in prosperity. You need to put in your sweat and tears in the form of thinking, planning and execution towards your goal. However, even then it may not work out. Some mysterious forces — what is commonly known as luck — also play a major role in making one triumph. It is a 50/50 partnership; do your part and let God/the universe take care of the rest.

To have the blessings of the divine on his side, Chanakya had the habit of invoking various deities before he started anything new, be it a battle or writing a book. In modern times, people may not believe in Godly intervention, but paying respect and gratitude to forces beyond human understanding has only helped generations to move ahead with time.

🐎 Conquer yourself to remain unbeatable

"Your mind is your best friend and your greatest enemy," says Shri Krishna in the *Bhagavad Gita*. Self-control is not easy to achieve and you will discover that the most difficult person to control is yourself. It may take years to discipline yourself, but once you have managed to get a grip on your emotions, nothing will be difficult for you.

"To remain indomitable, we need to conquer ourselves," says Chanakya in the *Arthashastra*, Book 1, Chapter 6, Indriya Jaya. If a king achieves *indriyajaya*, he will become a *vijigishu* (world conqueror). In the path to success, both the biggest hurdle and the biggest support is your own mind, depending on how you have trained it.

♞ Leaders take the final call

Opinions are given by everybody, experts give advice, and leaders take the final call. A good leader will know what the difference is between an opinion, advice and a decision. Opinions are something to be heard, but not necessarily to be taken seriously. Expert advice should be given due importance; these intellectual inputs make decision-making quite easy. But taking a decision is something only a leader can do. So if you are a leader, take the final call in a well thought out manner.

Chanakya knew that to make a leader into a good decision maker, he should have the necessary decision making skills. This includes alternative thinking, rational thinking, out of the box thinking and also creative thinking. One also needs to be trained in philosophical thinking, which includes the three foundations of Indian philosophies — *sankhya*, yoga and *lokayata*. All these dimensions put together make right decisions.

♞ Success should not lead to excitement

One should be poised in both success and failure. In failure, we get depressed and sorrowful, and in success we get elevated and excited. A leader should avoid any mood swings that can affect his mind. A calm mind is the most productive mind.

When one works hard towards success, it is only predictable to get carried away with positive results. Happiness is a natural feeling, and one should definitely be happy. But excitement is a state of mind that is not stable; one could do or say things in an exhilarated state and regret it later. A thrilled leader takes hurried decisions and jolts the whole system. A composed leader is the one who believes in a 'no jolts' policy.

♞ Do not give in to failure

Some people are blessed with a never-say-die attitude. They also face problems and challenges like the rest of us, but these people have tremendous willpower and persistence and they do not cower in front of hurdles. For them setbacks are temporary; they get up and get going towards their goals. Failure is not acceptable for them; they will always make a comeback.

Chanakya was also a man with tremendous resolve. He did not have an support from anyone; he walked the path towards his visions alone. When his father was murdered by

King Dhanananda, he had to run away from Pataliputra to Takshashila. However, he worked hard to make a comeback. When he was prepared, he defeated Dhanananda through his pupil Chandragupta Maurya and ended the Nanda dynasty altogether. He lived a purposeful life and became a role model for generations to come.

Strategy is more important in leadership than position

The one who has a plan is a leader, whether he has an official title or not. Having the title of a leader without knowing what to do with it is as good as having a house without keys. Strategists are the true leaders; their power comes from their intellect. These strategic thinkers actually rule the world; others are mere puppets in their hands. Instead of sitting on the chair themselves, they create the chair where the powerful sit.

HAVING THE TITLE OF A LEADER WITHOUT KNOWING WHAT TO DO WITH IT IS AS GOOD AS HAVING A HOUSE WITHOUT KEYS. STRATEGISTS ARE THE TRUE LEADERS.

Chanakya controlled the whole of united India just with his acumen. He was a strategist who kept his every move a secret. When the right time came, he played his cards. A patient thinker, there was nothing that he could not achieve once his eyes were set upon something.

🐎 Every detail matters

A house is made by cementing brick upon brick. Even
if there is one weak link, the whole house will collapse.
Therefore, when building the foundations of a country
or organization, be careful of every little factor, because
everything matters. Working with specifics can be boring,
but in the end, it will be worth to have a blemish-free
project. So spend time going over the minutiae.

When Chanakya wrote the *Arthashastra*, he went into the
finer details of everything. How to model a king, selection of
ministers, appointment of priests, administration, framework
of the law, creation of revenue, setting up industries,
deciding salaries, international policies, war strategies... the
list goes on. All this is given in the 6000 sutras he wrote. But
at the end of it, when all the details were implemented, he
created a formidable empire — Bharat.

🐎 Look at the tree and the forest

Some people get so much into details that they forget the
objective. Some others only look at the objective and forget
the details. The right approach is to look at the big picture
and also at the particulars. Leadership is about taking care
of the macro and the micro together.

Chanakya knew that for achieving the vision that he had
for Chandragupta Maurya's empire, he had to look into the
details. When there is a war, every soldier counts. Then,

the motivation level of the soldiers matters. Next they need to have enough weapons and ammunition. Finally, the war strategy — how to defeat the enemy comes into the picture. That is why the *Arthashastra* talks about every fine detail regarding war and its preparation (Book 7-14 war chapters). Make sure not to omit any details, however minor, when you map out your goal.

♘ No one is permanent

Built to Last: Successful Habits of Visionary Companies by Jim Collins and Jerry I. Porras talks about the principles behind great lasting organizations. Visionary leadership is what all these establishments have in common. Great leaders know that no one is permanent in the system, including the leader himself, but the organization should be able to withstand the test of time.

If you create something with this in mind, your creation will endure the test.

In his days, Chanakya built great institutions. Not only did he create an empire, he also created financial institutions, educational institutions, military institutions, industries and legal systems that would last forever. He made sure these institutions also moved forward at every level, from

> **GREAT LEADERS KNOW THAT NO ONE IS PERMANENT IN THE SYSTEM, INCLUDING THE LEADER HIMSELF, BUT THE ORGANIZATION SHOULD BE ABLE TO WITHSTAND THE TEST OF TIME.**

good to great. Refer to the *Arthashastra* to understand how
he built these amazing, reputed institutions.

♘ Play the game to win or do not bother

You never win a silver medal, you always lose a gold
medal. This is the reality. Most of us like to compromise
on our success. Coming in the second position in a race is
accepted as winning, but that is not real victory. There is a
big difference between No 1 and No 2. So go for gold and
only gold, not even silver. So if at all you want to play the
game, play to win it. If you are not sure, do not play; go back
and prepare, practice and come back with a strategy to win.

Chanakya wanted all his students to be No 1 in their
respective fields. *Vijigishu* is the word used for an ideal
leader as per the *Arthashastra*. Fire in the belly and a never-
say-die attitude is crucial if you want to be a leader. If you are
already a leader then face your next challenge, after that, go
for the next. Never stop until there is no one ahead of you.
You will be then leading the others.

♘ Be known to others, yet remain
unknown

Most authors have an advantage. They are known, yet also
remain anonymous. So they can enjoy the popularity of the
masses, without their privacy being encroached upon, like a

film star or a sports person. They can easily walk on the road during broad daylight and still enjoy the solitude.

Chanakya was very popular during his days, and yet he was unknown to the masses. He could walk into the market place and interact with the shopkeepers just like any other common man. At the same time, he could walk into any palace and get a royal welcome from the king. This quality to remain known when required and unknown otherwise keeps you sane and grounded; helps to have a balanced approach in life.

♞ A person belongs to a family

Whenever you are associating with a new person, check his background thoroughly. A person's upbringing can reveal a lot about his mindset.. One of the ways to know more about a person is to find out about his family; family values reflect a person's upbringing. Upbringing shapes ones personality in the long run.

Chanakya did that with Chandragupta Maurya. Though he noticed leadership qualities in him as a child, he also made sure that he validated his family circumstances. So he looked at the horoscope and checked Chandragupta's *kula*, *gotra*, etc. By doing this, Chanakya came to know about the boy's genetic imprint. Next, he met the mother of Chandragupta, and after he was fully convinced that the boy was worth his effort, he trained him to become one of the greatest kings of India.

♞ Be industrious, not greedy

"The world has enough for everyone's need but not enough for everyone's greed," said Gandhi. He was right because there is a big difference between need and greed. The real needs of a person are very few. But greed is limitless. Greed for money, power, name, fame or anything is dangerous. It can destroy you and others around you. However, one should not be lazy either, but industrious. A hardworking person is a blessing because others around him stand to benefit from his productivity.

The *Arthashastra* deals with power. And the true power of a king is his ability to make his people happy. This is spot-on for leaders, too. How can this be achieved? First of all, the basic needs of citizens/workers should be fulfilled — food, clothing, housing and other rudimentary requirements have to be dealt with. After that, one should also proceed to provide more and more for the good of others. Enterprising people bring peace and prosperity to others.

♞ Love transforms while lust destroys

Love is a poorly understood concept. Many people think that it is only physical in nature but in truth it is much beyond that. There is love between parents and children, among family members and also among friends. There is divine love between a devotee and God. However, one of the most important associations in India is the love between a *guru* and his *shishya*, a teacher and a student. This kind of love has the power to transform people. On the other hand, lust destroys everything, including a person's reputation and standing in society.

ONE OF THE MOST IMPORTANT ASSOCIATIONS IN INDIA IS THE LOVE BETWEEN A GURU AND HIS SHISHYA. THIS KIND OF LOVE HAS THE POWER TO TRANSFORM PEOPLE.

The affection between Chanakya and Chandragupta, the famous teacher and his student, is unique in Indian history. Chanakya transformed an ordinary village boy into an emperor of India. Apart from his advanced and well-planned training methods, it was also his unconditional love for his student that helped the whole process. Also Chanakya was careful about Chandragupta not developing a lust for power. This is documented in the *Arthashastra*.

♞ Pay your advisors

There are many ways to show respect. Imagine you have somebody working for you for several years. That employee's dedication and the time he has invested in your wellbeing is incomparable. Now, will it look good on you if you do not pay this person well? Compensating him poorly is equal to disrespecting his hard work. Pay your employees well and take care of their needs. In the same way, pay your advisors handsomely for their efforts in helping you with your dilemmas.

Chanakya made sure that his counselors were paid properly. In the *Arthashastra*, you can find the salaries of people employed by him (in the section about setting up of revenue by the administrator). Experts from every field used to guide the king. And the king made sure that these advisors were treated well and looked after with respect. Those who advise you are thinking of your benefit. In the same manner, you should also take care of their wellbeing.

♞ Giving money is a way of showing respect to others

Giving money to others is not about throwing your money at them grudgingly or with no care in the world. One must always make payments with love and gratitude. When we donate with such feelings in our heart, those at the receiving end will automatically feel nice. They will also feel respected. This kind of giving brings back to us the money, multiplied. It is not just the physical money that comes back, but you also receive blessings and good merits that will help your spiritual growth in return.

The concept of *guru dakshina* is popular in our culture. *Guru dakshina* is not just a fee; it is not just a monetary transaction. It is a way for the student to give back to his teacher — for the love, knowledge and wisdom he received under the guru's tutelage. Nobody can pay their teacher back, yet one needs to try his best to show his respect for his guru. Chanakya had educated Chandragupta, and the former had to give back to his teacher with respect, by making him the prime minister and the chief administrator of the Maurya Empire. Sometimes the payment can be in kind (money), sometimes in other forms. But do give back; it is every student's duty towards his tutors.

Never take a decision alone

Many people like to make decisions on their own. However, when it comes to a leader, such a practice can be risky. Even in the most desperate of situations, it is better to consult another person or two before taking a call. That is the reason why Chanakya wanted kings to be surrounded by their advisors and consultants. "In an urgent matter, he should call together the councilors as well as the council of ministers and ask them for their advice. What the majority among them declare or what is conducive to the success of the work, that he (leader) should follow," says Chanakya in the *Arthashastra*.

PEOPLE LIKE TO IMAGINE THINGS; MOSTLY THEY DO THIS BY IGNORING THE REALITY. IMAGINATION IS GOOD, BUT VERIFYING A SITUATION WITH FACTS IS EVEN MORE IMPORTANT.

People like to imagine things; mostly they do this by ignoring the reality. Imagination is good, but verifying a situation with facts is important. For instance, if somebody wants to start a business, it is quite natural that he may imagine all the factors that will lead to the success of his business.

To be positive about an idea is wonderful. However, it is better to consult a couple of experts before building on a new idea because no business is smooth and simple. Having consultants/advisors is a sure-shot way to learn about possible roadblocks on the way and plan ahead to avoid them on the journey to success.

♞ Do not take away the livelihood of the needy

There are needy people and there are greedy people. The greedy will not be satisfied with anything; even if they are given a lot of wealth, they will still want more. The needy are the ones who struggle for their basic survival. They need support and help. If you are running an organization, make sure that you do not take away the livelihood of the needy. They are dependent on you. Take care of them and in turn they will take care of your work.

Chanakya was a brilliant economist and his economic models had a humane approach. He took into consideration every section of the society. Some people are productive and efficient while some are lazy. And there is another type who are not productive, not because of their laziness but because of their limits. These people need to be looked after, mentored. A good example for Chanakya's thoughts about helping the needy is his mandates regarding the families of dead soldiers. The *Arthashastra* says, *"Of those dying while on duty, their sons and wives shall receive food and wages. And their minor children and the old and the sick should be helped. And he (the king) should grant them money and do the honours on occasions of death, illness and birth ceremonies."*

♞ Maintain your connections

A leader has to maintain relationships, not just within the family but also with his friends and allies. Chanakya in the Saptanga Model of a kingdom gives importance to *mitra* (a friend or an ally). Now, friends do not become close just like that. One has to put in effort and time to develop ties. To have long-lasting friendships, one needs to connect with the other person on an emotional level.

In life, people come and go. However, it is important to maintain relations with even those who have gone out of your life. In India, it is a tradition to remember even the dead and the departed every year through the ritual of *shraddha*. What about those who are alive? Remember them and make them feel wanted. Only then you will be valued as a good human being who will stick by his dear ones through thick and thin. And a leader's strength comes from his followers, his allies.

> ONE HAS TO PUT IN EFFORT AND TIME TO DEVELOP TIES. TO HAVE LONG-LASTING FRIENDSHIPS, ONE NEEDS TO CONNECT WITH THE OTHER PERSON ON AN EMOTIONAL LEVEL.

♞ Read people, study people, work with people

Scriptures tell us not to judge people, to accept all as equals. However, at the worldly level, we need to develop the quality to judge people. On a day-to-day basis, we deal with different types of people. And it is important that we know how to understand their personalities and figure out the best way to work with each one of them. For this, it is vital to understand human behaviour.

Chanakya was a teacher beyond excellence because he knew the art of decoding people; he used the critical thinking or *aanvikshiki* to achieve this. He could judge persons based on their behaviour, their words and deeds. And then he would look at their efficiency. For instance, if a person is not too intelligent but has a good build, he would recruit that person at a junior position in the military. If a person showed an inclination towards studies, he would place him as a university teacher. Thus, he always managed to recruit the right person for the right job.

♞ Know your duty and others' too

Never cross your limits. We generally tend to have an opinion about what others should be doing. On the contrary, each of us should know what we ought to be doing and just focus on making our work excellent, individually. By sticking to our individual roles, we will be creating a fully functional organization and a nation that is highly productive. So know your duty and know the duty of others, which is not your business. But yes, do help others with their workload if they ask you to.

WE GENERALLY TEND TO HAVE AN OPINION ABOUT WHAT OTHERS SHOULD BE DOING. ON THE CONTRARY, EACH OF US SHOULD KNOW WHAT WE OUGHT TO BE DOING AND STICK TO IT.

Chanakya had full clarity about his duty and the duty of others. That is why he wrote the *Arthashastra*, where everyone's role is clearly defined. His own calling was to teach as he was an *acharya* and a *shikshak*, and he guided others, like the king, to perform their responsibilities. Chanakya himself did not cross his limits to become a king neither did he allow others to cross theirs. During Chanakya's time, each person in the Maurya Empire performed his duty well for the welfare of the Empire.

🐴 Know the elephant (strengths) and understand its move (direction)

An elephant is a huge animal. Elephants were considered one of the biggest assets of any king's army. The study of the elephants is a subject in the *Arthashastra*, also there was a government department for their maintenance and wellbeing. During those days, it was important to understand these beasts and the strength they came with. But along with that, it was also vital to understand their moves so that mahouts could steer the animals where they want them to go. A rogue elephant is a danger to its owner.

Similarly, in every organization or kingdom there will be many powerful people. As a leader, one should know their strengths; they are like elephants. If these great people are not shown the right path, they can become destructive. So utilizing their potential in the right way is very critical to the success of any organization/kingdom. Without clear purpose, these talented people can become a nuisance and wreak havoc, just like wild elephants.

♞ Duty of a teacher

Teachers in India are the most respected people. But unfortunately, not many of them understand the responsibility that comes along with their position. Today, most people look at teaching as just another profession. But the very essence of teaching is much beyond being just a lecturer in a college or university. So if we were to look back, our ancient *rishis* would surely shout out to our generation's teachers: "Oh teacher! Know our duty, know your responsibility."

Chanakya's clarion call to his generation is relevant in our generation, too: "Wake up, teachers. The future of the nation belongs to you." Chanakya's life is inspiring to everyone, but most importantly to the teaching community. Chanakya was a model teacher. He knew the importance of theories. But he also understood that more important is the practice of the theories that one teaches and preaches. And finally he wrote a book, the *Arthashastra*, which became a textbook for all students.

♞ Have diversified income

People get stuck in life for various reasons. One of them is financial constraints. Some people are fully dependent on their jobs for running their families. Others do business to make a living. However, the smart ones are those who have diversified source of income. This way, even if one source dries up, you are left with other resources to maintain your home and other basic necessities.

Chanakya was one such person who created multiple channels of revenue for the kingdom. For instance, he understood that the treasury cannot be dependent only on agriculture for the taxes. If there was a drought or flood, it will affect the income generated. So he collected taxes from mines, factories and even from traders and other businesses. A smart person knows that a diversified financial plan will keep you risk-free.

♞ Informers are your strengths

What is information? It is the very source based on which leaders are able to take decisions. Information could be right or wrong, so it has to be verified. But without the latest, one cannot move things forward. Therefore, information and informers are the strengths of the leaders, the decision makers. Therefore, having a strong intelligence network is very much required for any organization or country.

Chanakya knew very well the necessity of information. He was adept at creating a network to collect news from around the kingdom and beyond, and based on that taking the right decisions for the benefit of the nation. In *Arthashastra*, there is a complete section on informers; they are the spies (Book 1, Chapter 12, Rules for Secret Servants). Without spies, it was impossible for a king to know what was happening in various parts of his kingdom or about the threats to his throne. Similarly, in an organization, the leader or CEO has to have his ear to the ground and have people to report directly to him about the goings-on inside the institution so that he is aware of each and every aspect of his company to lead it better.

Serve the country to reach God

To realize God is the ultimate goal of human existence. But what is the best way to reach Him? There are various ways given in our ancient Indian scriptures. A very popular method among them is Karma Yoga — the path of selfless action. But is it possible for a common man to do selfless deeds? Selfless action calls for a higher purpose; something that is beyond oneself. Therefore, one way to achieve this is by serving your country.

Chanakya was a nation builder. He worked his whole life serving his motherland. He created Bharat as a very rich and successful country. In this process, there were various hurdles, but he overcame all the challenges, and kept moving forward. In those ups and downs, he never lost sight of the purpose — nation-building. Finally when he achieved it, he retired from public life, retreated to the forest to indulge in spiritual quest and find God.

♞ Use alternative routes to reach your goal

There should be one goal, but there should be many routes to reach that goal. One of the mistakes that people make is that they have various goals but no clarity on how to fulfil those goals — the process is not clear, the route is undefined. While moving towards the goal, make sure you have alternative routes or backup plans. So if you get stuck on one direction, you can choose another way to reach the same goal. Stop not till you achieve your goal.

Chanakya's mind was always on an overdrive when he went out to conquer his enemies. His enemies were also equally smart. So he was continuously thinking of alternative methods to defeat the enemy. We find in the *Arthashastra* this kind

WHILE MOVING TOWARDS THE GOAL, MAKE SURE YOU HAVE ALTERNATIVE ROUTES OR BACKUP PLANS. SO IF YOU GET STUCK ON ONE DIRECTION, YOU CAN CHOOSE ANOTHER TO REACH THE GOAL.

of alternative thinking (Books 7-14 — war-related topics). The idea is to keep your mind alert and active. Imagine the enemy is smart, and so you have to be smarter than the enemy. Therefore, thinking ahead and thinking far is the path to success.

♞ Distractions are natural, but do not forget your goal

Once you decide on a goal, do not turn back. Set out on the journey with no other purpose but to win. Unwavering determination is an essential quality of a winner, and also a crucial leadership quality. If you have to, burn the bridges behind you. When you have no choice but to win, you cannot even think of failure. Distractions are natural in the journey towards success, but do not forget the goal for which you have started out.

When Chanakya wanted to defeat Alexander the Great, who was on his way to conquer the world, he did not get any support from other kingdoms. In fact, he managed to garner various opponents because of his ambitious plan. People doubted his intentions, criticized him and even insulted him. But he did not stop nor forget his goal. And finally, after his relentless pursuit, he got the help he needed. He collaborated with other Indian kings and kingdoms and defeated Alexander, thus achieving his goal.

♞ Take breaks, but do not stop your work

Life is a long journey; and you require a lot of energy and stamina to continue on this long journey. You can undertake this journey in two ways — run like a sprinter or like a marathoner. A sprinter uses up all his energy at one go. He has a short distance to cover and has to run fast. On the other hand, a marathoner proceeds slow but steady. He also has a long distance to cover.

Chanakya was a marathoner. He believed in the long term. So, he took his time, planned every detail before he started his journey. He went on relentlessly but he also took breaks. These breaks are essential to get some rest and start again, for energizing yourself. It is like filling the petrol tank of your car from time to time on a long drive. This method helped Chanakya accomplish a lot in his life. He shares his advice regarding breaks with his students in the *Arthashastra*, in Book 1, Chapter 19, Daily Routine of a King.

♞ When you work for others, others work for you

Life is all about give and take. But first you have to give. When you give something to someone, it will always come back to you as a reward. I am not talking about transactional activity here. But every action has an impact. So when you work for others, others also work for you. It is the law of the universe. If you are a selfish leader, then your followers also become selfish. So create a work culture in your organization where everyone thinks of a win-win situation and works for the benefit of all.

Chanakya spoke about work ethics in Book 7, Chapter 16 of the *Arthashatra*, Conduct of a King. He also understood that it all begins with the leader, at the top. Leaders create work culture in organizations; it is always a top-down approach. When the leader is working for the benefit of others, others work for the leader. Ashoka, the grandson of Chandragutpa, Chanakya's pupil, was a leader who worked to spread Indian wisdom across the globe. Later, others took his work forward, making him a global phenomenon.

Even the ignorant value great leaders

IF YOU ARE ABLE TO LEAD THE CLASSES AND THE MASSES AT THE SAME TIME, YOU ARE A POPULAR LEADER. CHANAKYA KNEW HOW TO CONNECT WITH THE SOCIETY.

Leadership is not just about leading the people whom you know, or those who understand your thought and philosophy. Leaders are the ones who not only have an intellectual connect, but also an emotional connect with their people. This connect is so strong that even the simple-minded and uneducated start to value the leader. That is what makes a leader great. If you are able to lead the classes and the masses at the same time, you are a popular leader.

Chanakya knew how to connect with all the people in the society. He also trained his kings to value all types of people. We see in the *Arthashastra* that he classified the people in the kingdom into various groups, and then he took care of each of these groups. *"He (the king) should provide one making a new settlement with grains, cattle, money and other things,"* says Chanakya in the *Arthashastra*. Some of these groups were poor and illiterate. But once this underprivileged section of the society was taken care of, even those people valued the leaders.

🐴 You are a leader

Yes, you are a leader. Do not believe it? Think! Yes, you are a leader to someone. Even if it is to just one person or a small group of people, you are still a leader. There are people who look upto you; they admire you either openly or silently. Leadership quality in people sometimes shows through without warning, during unpredictable times — when you take up some responsibility and take charge when no one is taking the lead. With that sense of accountability, the leader in you is born.

If you start studying the *Arthashastra*, you are sure to get some leadership ideas, and if you persist slowly these ideas will become a part of your personality and soon you will start to think like a leader. Further, the *Arthashastra* also gives you the tools that are required for a leader to plan, organize and carry on the work to its successful completion.

From thinking like a leader to becoming a successful leader, Chanakya shows the way.

♞ Leaders are incomplete without followers

What are leaders without any followers? It is the followers who actually make a leader. It is like a teacher is a teacher only because a student exists. The student comes first and therefore you become a teacher. Similarly a leader is a leader because there are followers. Look at M.K. Gandhi, he had no formal political position or designation, yet he was a popular leader because he had numerous followers.

WHAT IS DEAR TO HIMSELF IS NOT BENEFICIAL TO THE KING, BUT WHAT IS DEAR TO THE SUBJECTS IS BENEFICIAL (TO HIM).

Chanakya therefore created leaders from the dimensions of the followers. According to the *Arthashatra*, "*In the happiness of the subjects lay the benefit of the king and in what is beneficial to the subjects is his own benefit. What is dear to himself is not beneficial to the king, but what is dear to the subjects is beneficial (to him).*" Therefore, the first dimension is the people. A king exists because there are subjects. The support of the people is necessary. And taking care of his people is the first and foremost responsibility of any leader.

♞ Death cannot conquer a visionary

Leaders die, but their visions live on. Their ideas are carried forward from one leader to another, from one generation to the next. Leaders are beyond death, because visions are not just limited to the physical body. For example, there are organizations that have survived the test of time. Swami Vivekananda created the Ramakrishna Mission. This organization still continues to grow in spite of Swami Vivekananda's demise more than a century ago.

Chanakya was a thought leader. He lived a great life. Even after his death, the ideas of Chanakya, his vision, have lasted. The fact that you are reading this book today means there is something about Chanakya that has survived all these years. Death could not conquer Chanakya, because his vision lives on till today. The *Arthashastra* is a living example of this; it is still read, studied and applied even by modern-day leaders.

♞ Make God your partner

Who is a partner? A partner is someone who is an integral part of your project, company or even your life (your spouse is your life partner). We always look for an 'ideal' partner who can add value to the work we do. So, who is the best partner you can have for any undertaking? None other than God himself. God is the master of the universe. Once you make him your partner, how can you ever fail?

IT IS NORMAL IN INDIA TO INVOKE GOD BEFORE UNDERTAKING ANY MAJOR ACTIVITY. IT IS AN ASSURANCE THAT WITH DIVINE BLESSINGS, THE PROJECT WILL BE SUCCESSFUL, DESPITE THE HURDLES.

It is quite normal in India to invoke God before undertaking any major project or activity. It is an assurance that with divine blessings, the project will be successful, despite all the hurdles. In the beginning of the *Arthashastra*, Chanakya invokes God and his gurus to seek their blessings with an opening prayer, *"Om Namah Sukra Brahaspati Abhyam"*. And look at the success of the *Arthashastra* — a book that has become a bestseller of all times!

🐎 Leaders mix with commoners but do not become common

There is something elusive about leaders. If you observe any prominent figure in any field, you will notice that they all have the flexibility to be common and extraordinary at the same time. A person cannot be called a leader if he just sits at the headquarters issuing orders. He has to go down to the masses and understand their problems and yet stand out among them.

In the *Arthashastra*, Chanakya says that every leader should interact with the public. But he also goes on to clarify that a leader has to understand the problems of the commoners and solve them, but not get carried away. The beauty of the message is, 'Be with them, but stand apart.'

♞ Lift your people to the next level

Who is a leader? A leader is someone who lifts you up from your present status to the next, higher level. If you have been serving in the same post for a long time, then either you do not know what growth is, or you are in the wrong company. Be associated with great leaders who provide you with a purpose in life. This purpose will keep you going. The day you realize that you need to rise higher in life, you, too, become a leader.

Chanakya lifted a common boy, Chandragupta, to the highest level of becoming the emperor of a united India. But that is just one example. He also boosted the whole country to the next level. India, under Chanakya's guidance, became the richest country in the world. Imagine the impact it had on the people. When a country prospers, every citizen also grows to the next level. And everyone benefits. This is the real duty of a leader and thinker — to lift your people to the highest level.

♞ Honour scholars and thinkers

Every society has its own set of intellectuals. They are the thinkers, scholars, poets, artists and teachers. They are the ones whose main role is to apply their knowledge to shape a better society. These scholars and thinkers should be honoured and respected. They may seem like rebels with their sometimes outrageous ideas and concepts, but they are the truth-seekers. Intellectuals like to challenge everything and everyone in the process of seeking answers, and a good leader should not fear challenges.

In Book 13 of the *Arthashastra*, we find that when a king takes over another kingdom, he is advised to respect the scholars, thinkers and the elderly of that kingdom now under his command. Usually when there is a takeover, people of the rival territory are harassed and butchered. But Chanakya says to show them honour and respect because it is very necessary to establish a good social order.

♘ Be contented but not satisfied

There is a big difference between satisfaction and contentment. Their meanings are usually mixed up and used. A satisfied person will not have any more hunger. He will not have the drive to do anything further while a contented person is happy with himself. One should not be satisfied but be contented; one should have the drive to do more and more while being contended with the reward.

Chanakya was once such person who was totally content. Whatever he got as a *guru dakshina* from his students was enough for him. He was not greedy. But he was not satisfied and did not accept mediocrity. He always wanted the best for his nation. While contentment is a spiritual quality, not being satisfied keeps the human race going forward in search of excellence.

◥ Laziness is the route to destruction

If one is lazy, he will not only lose the current prosperity but future opportunities as well. "Be ever active in the management of the economy because the root of wealth is economic activity; inactivity brings material distress. Without an active policy, both current prosperity and future gains are destroyed," says the *Arthashastra*. Laziness is a dangerous attitude to have. It takes away everything you have earned. And also whatever is due will never happen because of your laziness. They say laziness settles as a guest in our minds and becomes the owner of the house. So do not let it take shelter in your mind, or it will lead to your downfall.

Chanakya never wanted his king to lead a lazy life. He was always active and wanted his students also to be that way. The kind of activity that is purpose-driven will lead to success in life. Being ever active is important. Leaders have to do multiple things at the same time. So if you complete the task at hand, immediately get on to the next one and so on. This kind of continuous action like a live wire will also inspire others around you.

◥ Leaders cannot lose hope; they are the only hope for others

Lord Ganesha, or Ganapati, is one of the most popular gods in India. 'Gana' means a group and 'pati' means leader. So the elephant-headed god is considered as the leader of a group. There are many things that we can learn from

IN EVERY CHALLENGING SITUATION, A LEADER SHOULD INSPIRE PEOPLE TO FIGHT AND EMERGE AS WINNERS.

Ganesha. One of the most important qualities is to keep the mouth shut and digest every problem. Therefore, he has a small mouth and a large belly. In the same way, a leader has to display a calm demeanour and never lose hope in any situation.

The leader is the only hope for his followers. If the leader loses hope, whom will people look up to? Therefore, in every challenging situation, a leader should inspire people to fight and emerge as winners. Chanakya says, *"If the king is energetic, his subjects will be equally energetic. If he is slack (and lazy in performing his duties) the subjects will also be lazy, thereby, eat into his wealth. Besides, a lazy king will easily fall into the hands of the enemies. Hence, the king should himself always be energetic."* This shows that a leader has to be self-motivated and is expected to take charge and take full responsibility for his actions.

♞ Do not underestimate your enemy

It is natural to fear someone who is bigger than yourself. If an elephant suddenly comes in front, any human being will get frightened, just by the size of the elephant. But also remember to not take people who are smaller than you in size for granted. Your biggest enemy may not be bigger than you, they could be smaller than you. An ant is very tiny. But this same ant can enter inside an elephant's ear and wreak havoc.

Chanakya gives us a similar warning in the *Arthashastra*. He wants the king to prepare for a fight against a large enemy, but also not to take his small enemy for granted (Book 12, chapter concerning the weaker king). Sometimes wars are not won only due to the size of the army but also due to the strategies that are applied. Study the enemy well and make sure that you are ready even for attacks that can come from the rear end, not just from the front.

🐎 Small is big

A seed is small but the tree that comes out of it is big. Similarly, your ideas could be small, but the outcome of that idea can be really huge. The one who can see the big in the small is an intelligent person. A smart person is one who can identify the potential in any situation or person, however insignificant. Once we master that technique of seeing the unseen, we become the creators of wonders.

Chanakya had spotted Chandragupta when he was a small boy. But he also saw the potential in him. This potential was tapped at the right time under Chanakya's tutelage. The correct training made Chandragupta one of the greatest leaders of our country. Chanakya not only looked at potential kings, but also potential ministers and other people

who could run the kingdom in an effective manner. Good
teachers know how to do that, to turn the small into big.

Humility is strength, not a weakness

When we see a humble person, we think he is so because
he is weak. But that is a mistake. Humility is strength, not
a weakness. When Gandhiji started fighting against the
British, they wrote him off and his method of Satyagraha
as something that weak people do. But that simple looking,
unarmed philosopher made the mighty British Empire
come down on its feet. So when a person is humble, we
realize in the long run that he is truly a powerful person.

Chanakya wanted his leaders do develop humility. That
did not mean that he wanted his leaders to be weaklings.
When situation demanded, these humble kings fought the
greatest of wars and defeated the mightiest of enemies. True
strength comes from humility. Truly powerful people are
always humble.

Fear not the enemy

Do not fear your enemy. Because if you do, even before you
have started the battle, you have accepted defeat. Fear is a
mental state. And if you fuel it too much, there is a danger
of it becoming a reality. Fear makes the threat look bigger
than it actually is. How many people really die of snake bite?

In many cases, more than the poison of the snake, it is the fear and shock that kills the victim. So fear not and you will be victorious in anything you undertake.

The *Arthashastra* gives us various methods of fighting the enemy — *sama, dana, bheda* and *danda*. Chanakya advises us to choose a method according to the enemy. It also depends on the situation and the timing. The enemy may be big or small, the enemy may be new or old, you can surely defeat him. The way to do it is by first removing the fear from your mind. Only with a calm mind will you be able to win.

♞ Your anger is an advantage to your opponent

When we are angry, our judgement is clouded. We cannot think clearly. So when we are angry and out of control, it is an advantage to the adversary because our decisions will be flawed. Therefore, one needs to check his anger from time to time. Face it and let it not take control of you. Take control of your anger and win over it.

WHEN WE ARE ANGRY AND OUT OF CONTROL, IT IS AN ADVANTAGE TO THE ADVERSARY BECAUSE OUR DECISIONS WILL BE FLAWED. TAKE CONTROL OF YOUR ANGER AND WIN OVER IT.

In the chapters and books related to war in the *Arthashastra* (Books 7-14 related to war topics) we find that Chanakya also used anger as a tool to defeat the enemy. He instigated them and when they lost their capacity of judgement, they were attacked and defeated. Another method he used was to infuse rage into the people of the enemy kingdom. When the citizens are angered, it is very easy to overthrow the ruler. Make sure to keep your anger under control.

Everyone is useful

The most important war is sometimes won by the lowest soldier. In fact the army general knows that everyone in the army is useful. Not only those in the higher ranks, but also the bottommost in the ranks has some way to contribute to the winning of the war. So everyone is useful. A battalion does not just contain soldiers; they have a support system that go along with the fighters — the cooks, the doctors and even the priests.

In case of a war, Chanakya would map every type of person in the army, and use the right person for the right kind of attack. You do not need a king to kill another king. But at times, even a small solider can do the job in a very simple and effective manner. The real crux of the war is to send the right person to complete the right job.

When you set out to destroy, annihilate

Anything left behind, even if it is a seed, will grow back again. Therefore, it is not only important to defeat the

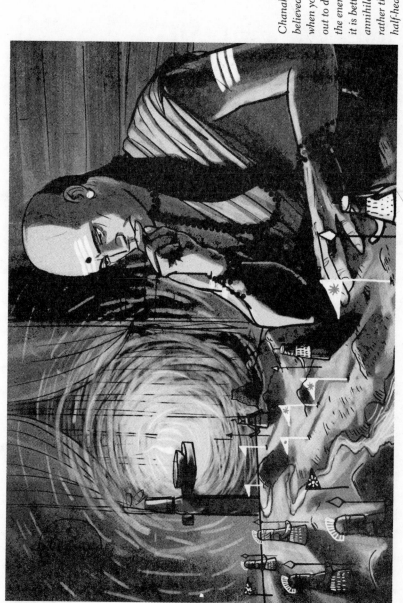

Chanakya believed that when you start out to destroy the enemy, it is better to annihilate rather than do a half-hearted job.

enemy but to end the hostility completely. Chanakya had a big challenge in front of him in the form of Alexander the Great. He had come to conquer India but Chandragupta Maurya, with the help of Chanakya's strategies, defeated him. However, Chanakya realized that Alexander's army would come back again to attack India. Therefore, he got Chandragupta married to a Greek noblewoman in order to bury the enmity forever.

In the same way, when you start something, some activity, some project, you must finish it. Something left pending can come back to haunt you. It is not about how many things you have started, but how many of those you have completed. Therefore, plan well and finish the work that you have started. If you do an excellent job, you leave a mark in the universe; future generations will remember your work, the way we remember Chanakya today.

♞ When you create something, build it to last

Most of us set out to do something out of impulse. But if we are going to create anything, we should do it with a long-term approach. A quality product will endure the test of time, just like some organizations and brands we have today. They are beyond people, they are time-tested and they have become the benchmark for others to follow. They are a proof of excellence. These institutions remind us that having strong foundations will set an example for many generations.

Chanakya was one such personality who built a nation to last. He knew that many of his ideas were incomprehensible to his generation. But he had a deeper understanding of how to leave a lasting contribution. These principles of long-lasting empires are given in the *Arthashastra*, Book 1, Chapter 3, Establishing the Vedic Lore. Follow Chanakya's methods and you will be building an empire or creating a project that will endure.

♞ Take guidance from astrologers

An astrologer can be wrong but not astrology. An astrologer is a human being and so his predictions can go wrong, however, astrology is a science based on mathematics and certain natural principles that are always accurate. The problem with most of us is that we trust our astrologer more than astrology. Choose a trustworthy astrologer for consultation; a person who has a deeper understanding of human behaviour is very important.

Indians formulated Vedic astrology, and Chanakya was one such expert who studied the subject thoroughly. He used to take decisions only after consulting the astrological charts. This is a very scientific process as well. It is about permutation and combinations, and mathematics has faultless rules that do not change. Take a look at astrology from the scientific angle.

♞ Nurture your relations

Many of us think that contacts are to be used only for a purpose. When the purpose is achieved and the work is over, these acquaintances are forgotten. This is not a good approach. One should keep the links forever, because you never know when these connections will be required again. And you may also be the contact point for someone else at some other time. Today with the help of technology it is easy to keep and maintain connections forever. But do not forget to add the human touch; it is very important even when you use technology.

"He should establish contacts with forest chieftains, frontier-chiefs and chief officials in the cities and the countryside," advises the Arthashastra. Even the king is instructed to maintain his relations with others. Both the subjects and the king require each other; it is an interdependent relationship. No one can sustain alone, whether it is a king or a CEO of an organization. Everybody needs support and cooperation to grow and flourish.

♞ Make strategic thinking a habit

What is the first thing you do when you wake up? In most traditions across the globe, one is supposed to pray and offer thanks to God for a wonderful day ahead. And next? Most people start worrying about the day ahead. However, Chanakya had an alternative: after your morning prayers, start pondering over the day ahead. This way, you start planning ahead for a great day and not just wish for it.

Chanakya wanted his students to develop strategic thinking as a habit. Habits are not formed overnight. They require time and effort. And once you develop this habit, it becomes a part of your personality; it happens unconsciously. Your mind becomes ready to take up any challenge that comes during the day. Get up, get ready, start planning ahead and be a winner every day.

If you were cheated, learn the lesson and become smart. Do not cheat others

When one was tricked in some way, it is natural to feel hatred towards the person who is responsible for it. However, that hatred does not have any benefit; it only leads to negativity. A better way is to learn a lesson from the episode and move on. At the same time, because you were hoodwinked does not mean you should do the same with others. Our basic nature of goodness should not change, no matter the circumstances.

In the annals of history, you will find many great sages and saints ill-treated by others. But these great men and women rose above the hatred and showered blessings on those miscreants so that the lives of those mere mortals were transformed. Chanakya's life itself was full of problems and challenges. His father was killed by King Dhanananda. But instead of hating him and killing Dhanananda, Chanakya used this opportunity to build a united India for future generations.

♞ Be gentle on yourself

Many of us feel that life is not fair when something horrific happens to us. But if you look around, life is most fair, because some or the other unfortunate incident is happening or has happened to everybody at some point or the other. When a tragedy hits, life is knocked out of balance. You may not be at your best during this period. It may take some time before you get back on your feet and carry on with life. Do not beat yourself up for not doing well immediately after. Just give yourself time. Once things settle down, with a calm mind, you can plan ahead.

> WHEN A TRAGEDY HITS, LIFE GETS KNOCKED OUT OF BALANCE. YOU MAY NOT BE AT YOUR BEST DURING THIS PERIOD. IT MAY TAKE SOME TIME BEFORE YOU GET BACK UP.

In the *Arthashastra*, there are two types of calamities mentioned — one that is created by human beings, like wars, riots, etc., and the other natural disasters, like earthquakes, floods and droughts. In either case, one should allow time to pass. And then analyze the situation and start all over again, with renewed vigour.

🐎 Silent does not mean stupid

People consider introverts as slow-witted because they do not speak much. Before you judge, these silent observers maybe the best thinkers around. Do not fall for the outward appearances. Look beyond what you see. Those who use their mind in a creative, logical and rational way may not use their tongue much. From silence one day may come words of influence.

Once, Chanakya was invited to the court of King Dhanananda. He sat silently among the great personalities, observing the proceedings at the court. Various scholars were immersed in philosophical discussions. Chanakya noticed that the king was not concerned or interested in these deliberations. He left the hall, making Dhanananda angry. The king insulted Chanakya, who in turn took an oath to dethrone the king. Finally when he achieved his goal through Chandragupta Maurya, Chanakya's silent message was: "Just because I am silent, it does not mean that I am stupid."

🐎 Do not anger the already enraged

When someone is angry, he is not in a good mental state. If you ever have to deal with an angry person, you should remain cool and level headed. If you also lose your composure, then there is no hope in that situation. Do not anger the already infuriated. It is like pouring oil onto the fire. It will only aggravate the situation and things will get out of control. So, the best way to tackle a situation involving an angry person is by placing your mind above your heart.

A calm leader is essential to tackle any eventuality. Therefore, Chanakya suggests that one should be able to control ones senses or *indriyajaya*. When the whole world is on fire, only a cool-headed person will be able to put out the fire. Fire cannot be doused by fire; it requires water to do the trick.

♞ Fear is a tool to control others

One should not be afraid of anything, but at the same, fear can be used to control other people, especially your rivals. In any sport, players use various strategies to win, and installing fear in the hearts of the opponents is a time-tested tactic. When afraid, people lose the ability to think clearly; it becomes easy to defeat them. But to induce alarm in someone, one needs to understand human psychology. Once you know the trepidation of your enemy, you can easily win the game.

Chanakya had a very interesting way of intimidating the enemy. He used to send spies into the enemy camp to spread the rumour that the native king is god-incarnate and any harm to him will bring bad luck to the opponent. This way, he used to sow the seeds of doubt in minds of the rivals. Slowly this doubt turns into fear and it is "game over" for the opponents.

♞ Greed is dangerous

Many people consider greed a driving force to accomplish more. Therefore, they believe that greed is good. This is a very wrong theory and very immoral approach. In fact, greed is dangerous. It will destroy all the things that you have achieved. Do not confuse between greed and ambition. If are ambitious for a larger purpose, it is very good. But if you are greedy and self-centred, it is damaging.

In the *Arthashastra*, Chanakya has elaborated on this fine distinction between being greedy and being ambitious. Every leader has to be ambitious (*vijigishu*) but greed is a vice. Chanakya advices to eliminate greed; many greedy leaders in the past have destroyed their kingdoms. On the other hand, an ambitious leader generates prosperity for everyone and is an inspiration to others. Get far away from greed.

♞ Do not pin your failures on others

When you fail at something, it is very easy to blame somebody else for it. These blame games are only excuses. Very few people would take the responsibility of failure on themselves. If we think carefully and analyze the situation, we will find that somewhere there was something lacking from one end due to which the failure happened. So, we should learn from failure and take the corrective step and move ahead. Try something different and march towards success.

One of the qualities of a leader is to achieve success in spite of the hurdles on the way, says the *Arthashastra*, Book 6, Chapter 1, Qualities of a King. Fortitude is another such quality of a leader that keeps him going. For that to happen, one should love his work and be ready to give his life to what he is doing. After all, when you commit your life to your work with love, there is nothing in the world that can stop you. All great achievers were single-mindedly focused on their goal and they finally fulfilled them.

ONE OF THE QUALITIES OF A LEADER IS TO ACHIEVE SUCCESS IN SPITE OF THE HURDLES ON THE WAY. LEARN FROM FAILURE AND TAKE THE CORRECTIVE STEP AND MOVE AHEAD.

Humour can be a solution

A complex situation can be resolved in various ways, if you apply your mind to it. Have you ever wondered that even humour can be a good solution to some very serious problems? Yes, it is true. If you are able to tackle the most disturbing situation in a witty manner, the whole atmosphere becomes light and tension-free. Swami Chinmayananda, the great spiritual master, went through a heart surgery. When he was told that his heart had expanded in size, he laughed it off saying, "Finally I am happy to know that I have a large heart."

Chanakya is known for being a serious personality, but he also had a great sense of humour. Though the *Arthashastra* deals with grave and important matters of wealth and governance, it also talks about how to lighten up situations. An example is the presence of a court jester in the king's life. The main work of the court jester is to keep the situation light and funny. But he also makes sure that deep within the laughter are some good messages. Life should be taken seriously, but make sure to have some fun along the way.

Master something difficult

Learning to ride the elephant is a difficult task. But once you have mastered it, you are a changed person. The elephant is a mighty animal. So if you know how to control the beast, you are mightier than the mighty. In the olden days, kings were taught to hunt, capture and domesticate pachyderms. This requires a good amount of skill. It is also a mental power play between the strength of the elephant and the brain of the human being.

Unlike the kings in olden days who had to hunt elephants and capture them, today a leader's role is considerably less tricky. However, it is still useful for the leadership skills of a person to learn something new or master something difficult. Be it a new language or an effective way to communicate with your employees, it is always good to be on top of your game with new knowledge and abilities.

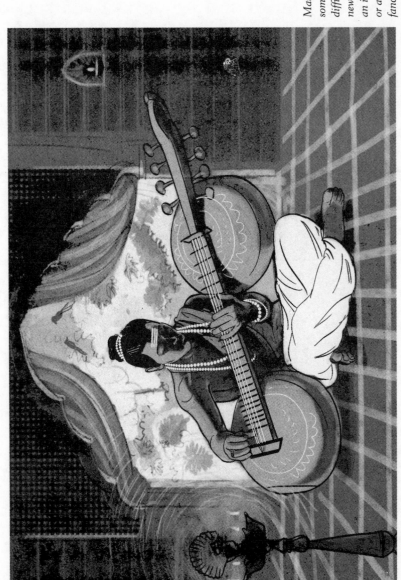

Master something difficult, be it a new language or an instrument or anything you fancy.

♞ An intoxicated driver crushes everything in the way

A driver is someone who guides and takes us on the journey. Having a good driver is an important part of the travel plan. If the driver knows the path very well, then the journey is smooth and enjoyable. Therefore, Arjuna selected Krishna as his chariot driver to steer him to victory in the *Mahabharata*. On the contrary, if the driver is irresponsible and intoxicated, he can create a lot of damage including crushing everything that comes in the way.

Who is our driver in life? Who shows us the way? A driver in the spiritual sense is someone who gives us direction, who helps us avoid pitfalls on the way. Trusted gurus or mentors play the role of a good driver in our lives. So choose them carefully. If Chandragupta Maurya had not accepted Chanakya as his guru, he would not have found a place in the history books. So if you want to be successful in life, find your Chanakya. He will lead you to success.

♞ Help each other

Elephants always move in groups. They live in a fission-fusion society. Studies show that they display emotions like sympathy for those suffering in their herd and try to help when any of their members is in trouble. Because these beasts are huge and strong, they can live as individuals and protect themselves. But they choose to live together.

The reason why a herd, when disturbed, is dangerous and difficult to defeat is because elephants look out for each other. Let us also be like elephants, strong individually but stronger collectively.

The most successful are the ones who are good at cooperating with others. In a world where networking leads to more opportunities and triumphs, loners are left in the dust to pick up after themselves. It is only by collaborating with others that you develop new ideas. For a leader, being in touch with other leaders and his own followers is essential for survival.

🐎 Make peace with reality

Nature balances everything. The laws of nature are perfect and once we understand them and are in tune with them, we will be able to live a life of balance. There may be certain aspects of nature that we do not like, but remember that they will always be there whether we want it or not. For example, most of us have a dislike towards snakes. And it is natural to fear and sometimes even hate them. But the reality is that snakes are a part of nature as much as we are and they will remain so.

In the same manner, Chanakya understood that nobody likes to have enemies. But the reality is that adversaries do exist. And it is important for us to manage them properly. In the Saptanga Model of a good kingdom in the *Arthashastra*, Chanakya also added the eighth part of a kingdom, called

'*Shatru*'. No one likes to have a *shatru* (enemy), but *Chanakya Niti* is all about managing your *shatru*.

Worship nature

Cow worship has been a part of Indian culture since eons. There is a traditional reason for that. In India, the first unit of society is family. And animals and birds of the family are also considered as family members. One such integral part of Indian families has been the cow. Since cow's milk is consumed in the households and is a major part of the diet, the animal is given the stature of mother and worshipped as well.

Chanakya, in the daily ritual of the king detailed in the *Arthashastra*, advises the king to start his day by giving salutations to the cow. It signifies two things — first, he is following the tradition of the ancestors. The second is that it shows respect to nature. Animals are a part of nature and man needs to live in harmony with nature. If there is imbalance in nature, the whole ecosystem will collapse. Therefore, a king must lead the way in respecting nature and the whole kingdom will follow suit.

> **ANIMALS ARE A PART OF NATURE AND MAN NEEDS TO LIVE IN HARMONY WITH NATURE. IF THERE IS IMBALANCE IN NATURE, THE WHOLE ECOSYSTEM WILL COLLAPSE.**

♞ Find the weakness of the competitor

There are many ways to win against your rival. The most important thing is to study the activities of the enemy before you take him on. Even in sports, if you want to win, not only should you prepare well but you should also know the weaknesses of the other players. Knowing the weakness of the enemy gives you a strategic advantage. Based on the way he thinks and behaves, you can plan your moves.

In the *Arthashastra*, Chanakya stresses the importance of scrutinizing the opponent. *"After ascertaining the relative strength or weakness of powers, place, time, revolts in fear, losses, expenses, gains and troubles, of himself and of the enemy, the conqueror should march,"* says the *Arthashastra*. This is gathering of intelligence. Once the information is collected then depending on the situation, you can plan your move. Planning is the first step to victory.

♞ Know the strengths of the opponent

Never take your adversary for granted. You could be a Goliath but your competitor could be a young David. Your strengths alone cannot make you victorious. At times, you lose because of your enemy's strength. Gauging his abilities gives you a lot of scope to make careful moves. How to turn the strength of the enemy into his weakness in itself is a war strategy.

Chanakya knew how to find out not just the weaknesses

but also the strengths of the enemy. He would deploy his informers and spies and based on the gathered information, would break the very backbone of the foe. He also had a robust system of *vishkanyas* (female spies) who would penetrate the enemy kingdom to find specific information. Chankya's secret was to know that in the strength lays the weakness.

♞ The leader will arrive

There are situations in life that are totally out of your control. In spite of your best efforts you may not be able to solve a problem. However, remember that there is hope in even the worst situations. Deep within every person there is a faith that things will improve. And it will happen when you have someone who comes into your life accidentlly or otherwise, and takes charge of the situation. This person who will turn around the whole scenario is the leader. And remember that one day the leader will arrive.

Dhanananda as a ruler was at the peak of his incompetence. Corruption, bad governance, public outcry and frustration were devouring the nation. And at the same time, an external force, Alexander the Great, was preparing to attack India. There

THERE ARE SITUATIONS IN LIFE THAT ARE OUT OF YOUR CONTROL. IN SPITE OF YOUR BEST EFFORTS, YOU MAY NOT BE ABLE TO SOLVE A PROBLEM. HOWEVER, REMEMBER THERE IS HOPE.

was little hope. But Chanakya knew that a good leader was required to ride out the crisis. And then, under the guidance of Chanakya, Chandragupta Maurya, the new leader, emerged. Under the leadership of Chandragupta, there was a turnaround in the governance of the kingdom and India witnessed one of her golden eras under the Maurya Empire.

🐎 Start something new, but always complete it

When power changes hands and a new leader arrives, there are always some new projects, some new initiatives. A good leader is not lazy and is someone who wants to leave his mark by doing something worth remembering, something of significance. This is why new leaders make promises and announcements as soon as they take up their charge. But just starting a new project or scheme will not make one a good leader. It is essential that what has been started must be completed as well.

Starting, executing and finishing a project successfully makes a great leader. Therefore, we find that in the *Arthashastra*, Chanakya gives guidance on how to start and complete a project. *"Others should not know about any work sought to be done by him. Only those who undertake it should know (about it) when it is begun or even when it is actually completed,"* says Book 1, Chapter 15, Verse 17. Nobody remembers any project only because it was initiated, but because it was carefully executed and completed on or before time. Therefore, time management also becomes key to leadership success.

♞ Continue good work

The best thing about good work is that you get more exposure and more opportunities to continue your efforts. Those who are efficient have a unique problem — more responsible work comes to them. This is the law of nature; once you start, you cannot stop. Therefore, if you are doing good work continue doing good work. When your work becomes God's work, there is a tremendous impact on yourself and the society. Your work is then no longer your work alone, it becomes an integral part of the world.

IF YOU ARE DOING GOOD WORK CONTINUE DOING GOOD WORK. WHEN YOUR WORK BECOMES GOD'S WORK, THERE IS A TREMENDOUS IMPACT ON YOURSELF AND THE SOCIETY.

Chanakya's life was about continuing good work. After he had accomplished the goal of making India one of the most powerful nations of the world, did he stop working? No, in fact he continued working towards the next level. He started writing the *Arthashastra*, a phenomenal contribution not only to his generation but for many generations to come. Later he continued teaching leadership lessons to students from across the globe. He was a mentor and leadership guru till his last breath.

♞ Remove the unrequired

We keep collecting things throughout our lives. Wherever we go, we buy something new — clothes, souvenirs, books, etc. Later, when we take stock, many of those items may have become junk, taking up valuable space. Every once in a while, it is important to de-clutter life and keep only those with us that are important and useful to us. This will help us lead a simple and organized life.

Chanakya was a great curator, a person who accumulated knowledge. He collected all that was available in his generation, all that was written by the previous scholars in the field of political science. There were many *Arthashastras* before Chanakya wrote his own *Arthashastra*. He collected and studied all the ageless principles of leadership and then penned his own *Kautilya's Arthashastra*. He weeded out what was archaic, retained what was necessary and came up with his own theories on governance.

♞ Take a walk in nature, work with nature

Stress is a buzzword for our generation. We have glorified stress to such an extent that we have a huge industry that operates in stress management, de-stressing, stress-free living, etc. But the reality is that every person in every generation goes through stress. There are many ways to tackle that stress. One of the important methods is to spend time with nature. When we work with nature, we truly become stress-free.

A walk in nature is something that is recommended by our ancient teachers. They knew that nature has a magical effect on our minds. It can elevate one's mood and lower stress. Chanakya, too, suggests in the *Arthashastra* that a daily walk is essential for a king. When we walk, it is not just a physical activity but also a mental activity. We get refreshed and are ready to work again with re-energized mind and body.

Natural laws do not change

Think about all the successful scientists, sportsmen, businessmen and leaders. You will find that they are successful because they work with certain natural laws in their respective fields. Scientists discovered certain phenomena. Sportsmen tune their bodies in order to make nature work for them, and businessmen understand some natural principles of wealth creation that make them successful. Thus one thing is sure that nature and natural laws are the same, they do not change. So once we understand that and tune ourselves to them, we are bound to succeed.

The Saptanga Model of the *Arthashastra* is also called *Prakriti* (nature). In Book 6, Chapter 1, Verse 1, it says, "*Swami, amatya, janapad, durga, kosha, danda, mitra, iti prakritiya.*" This model advocates that a successful kingdom can only be built keeping the seven parts together. It is a natural model of running a kingdom. This model is still relevant today because laws of nature do not change with time.

♞ Wisdom is not ancient, it is eternal

Chanakya was a wise man. He had a deep understanding of what worked and what did not. He used his intelligence for the benefit of the society and not just for selfish reasons. And in the process he discovered some timeless ancient knowledge and transformed it into the magnificent *Kautilya's Arthashastra*. Therefore, his wisdom is not dated, belonging to the 4th century BC, but eternal and relevant. His teachings will never expire.

The *Arthashastra*, even though written by Chanakya, in reality does not only include his ideas. It is a collection of ideas from the previous teachers of *Arthashastra* (political science), which he studied and modified as per the requirement of his generation. This means that every generation will have to find its own *Arthashastra*; study Chanakya and find those ideas that can be used today.

♞ You cannot avoid work

There is no choice but to slog. For many people, work is something that we do for a living. But that is only one type of work. Even if we take a break or go on a holiday, we still have to do somethings, like cooking food, paying bills, etc. Even when we are sleeping, our bodies are at work; we are breathing and our internal activities are going on. Like our internal organs, we must also choose to work for some higher cause and not just to make a living.

What is the duty of a leader? Why should a leader work? In the true sense, he should be functioning for the benefit of others and not for himself. True leaders work not for money or status, but for larger and nobler causes. Chanakya advised kings to work for the happiness of the subjects. *"In the happiness of the subjects lies the benefit of the king and in what is beneficial to the subjects is his own benefit. What is dear to himself is not beneficial to the king, but what is dear to the subjects is beneficial to him,"* says the *Arthashastra*, Book 1, Chapter 19, Verse 34.

WHAT IS THE DUTY OF A LEADER? WHY SHOULD A LEADER WORK? IN THE TRUE SENSE, HE SHOULD BE FUNCTIONING FOR THE BENEFIT OF OTHERS AND NOT FOR HIMSELF.

♞ Get enough rest

Work we should and rest we must. We must rest so that we can work better. However, too much rest can make one lazy. And once we have developed laziness, it is difficult to shake it off. So once fully rested, get back to work. Rest makes us refreshed and energetic. Without adequate rest, we will burn out and will not be able to work at our optimum efficiency.

Chanakya's prescribed routine for a king includes rest. According to Chanakya, a king should take a break in the afternoon for about one and a half hours. And at night, he can sleep for about four and a half hours. That is a total of six hours per day, a good amount of rest for an adult person. During the remaining hours, one must aim to work selflessly.

🐎 Thinking leads to creativity

How does one create anything? It is only through one's mind. All inventions, discoveries and creations have taken their shape as an idea or a thought. These ideas then take on their physical form after much hard work. Think of anything — a painting, a building, a book, a vaccine — all these were in the mind of the artist or the scientist. These were the thinkers who then became the creators. Therefore, thinking creates.

One needs to spend quality time thinking if one wants to create anything new. And the process of thinking should be taken very seriously. Thus *aanvikshiki*, the art of thinking, is discussed as the first subject in the *Arthashastra*. Chanakya begins with telling that it is important to spend every day a significant amount of time in creative and analytical thinking. That leads to success.

🐎 'Om' or the start

Om is not just a symbol of religious representation. It denotes eternity. Om is a combination of sounds 'A' 'U' and 'M'. A stands for the start, U stands for continuity and M stands for the end. Therefore, everything from start to end is contained in this one word called Om. Ancient scriptures have talked about the benefits of meditation or reflecting upon Om at length. Once we understand the real meaning of 'Om', everything else in life become simpler, clearer.

The *Arthashastra* starts with the word 'Om'. Chanakya invokes his teachers by saying, "*Om Namah Sukra Brahaspati….*" With putting Om in the beginning, he has invoked *all* the great teachers, the powers of the world and the blessings of all the gods. Om is also called the Pranav Mantra, an invocation that has lasting and eternal value — like the *Arthashastra* itself.

♞ Depth is important

In the depths of the ocean lay its secrets, but we only see the waves. However, a real sea voyager knows there are unlimited treasures to be discovered at the deep end of the sea. In the same way, life has a deeper meaning. We look at life only superficially. But depth is important. As we question the very essence, objective and purpose of life, we will find meaning to life that will lead us to fulfillment.

Chanakya's thoughts had depth. To look at the life of Chanakya as a story is missing the point. What he did is indeed impressive — the way he created an emperor out of

an ordinary boy, called Chandragupta; the way he defeated
Alexander the Great and how he made the nation wealthy.
But there is more to Chanakya than that. When you read
the *Arthashastra*, try to find those deep insights that went on
to make him a legend.

♞ Think about all possible angles

How to think? One should be able to think multi-dimension
and not just one way; from various angles and perspectives.
For instance, when we are building an organization, we
should construct in such a way that it should be 'built to
last'. This is possible only if we can think of in the long-
term. At the same time, we should be able to think in a
wider sense of its impact on the society and the changes it
will go through.

Chanakya had trained his disciples to think intensely. To
be able to think of the future is called visionary thinking
and it is all-inclusive thinking when one is able to think
of wide-reaching consequences of an action. The leaders
should be able to build nations that will survive the test of
time. Therefore, one of the important factors is economic
stability while building a nation. Chanakya built a new
India on strong economic and spiritual principles because
he understood the importance of thinking about all
possible angles.

♞ See the future, NOW!

Can you see the future now? We are not talking of clairvoyance. We are discussing 'insights' and 'impact' here. Every action has an impact. Visionary leaders and visionary companies know this. They do not wait for the future to happen; they plan for it in the present itself. They make the future happen. If you are able to see your future clearly and now, you are already taken the first step towards visionary leadership.

EVERY ACTION HAS AN IMPACT. VISIONARY LEADERS AND VISIONARY COMPANIES KNOW THIS. THEY DO NOT WAIT FOR THE FUTURE TO HAPPEN; THEY PLAN FOR IT IN THE PRESENT ITSELF.

While writing the *Arthashastra*, Chanakya was writing in all the three aspects of time. He was reflecting on the past — the way kingdoms were made successful, he was writing in the present — the way the present kingdoms are being ruled and he was writing in the future — he was visualizing the way ideal kingdoms of the future should be. Therefore, he could see the future as if it was happening right there and right in front of him.

♞ A circle is always complete

The word '*mandala*' is very common in the *Arthashastra*. There are many instances where it is also used for planning and strategy. Also there is a full book on Mandala Theory (The *Arthashastra*, Book 6, The Circle of Kings). Circle has two representations. One, it is endless; it doesn't have a start or an end. The other is that a circle is complete. It is full and therefore, it also reflects eternity.

Life is a circle. We are all a part of the circle of life. We come from dust and go back to dust. Water from the seas forms clouds and these clouds then pour down back as rain. So, from these circles, we also wonder and find the meaning to life. While life is like a circle (confusion), life is also about another circle (eternity). So let us move from the limited to the unlimited. From mortal to the immortal. From death to eternity.

♞ A circle is ongoing

In a circle, every point is the starting point and every point is the end point. One cannot make out where it starts and where it ends. This theory of beginning-less and endless phenomenon can be applied to every field. Indian spirituality also refers to this marvel as *anarambh* (beginning-less) and *ananth* (endless).

Chanakya knew that dynasties have their life spans. They have some beginnings and also various endings. But having studied these cycles of dynasties, he also came to certain conclusions. One can build a kingdom based on the eternal principles. Those principles of eternity in the form of circles are found in the *Arthashastra*, Book1, Chapter 1 — the way dynasties can become permanent. A wheel moves in circles, but still has a center that is permanent and immovable.

♞ Let others take over

People die, but organizations can last forever. This is the limitless within the limited. A person has only limited time on this earth and once the time is up, he has to leave. But an organization or institution can be limitless. It can last for hundred or even thousands of years. If you are a leader, you should know when to stop and let others take over your position, so that the organization can continue to grow. There is a saying, "Genius is about knowing when to stop."

While anointing Chandragupta as the king of Magadha, Chanakya knew that he was only a human being whose time is limited. It was important for him to create structures, systems and processes where other leaders can emerge, too, so that the legacy is carried forward. This is succession planning. Therefore, in the *Arthashastra*, Chanakya advises the king to step down and let the next generation take over the kingdom when the time comes. When a leader relinquishes his post on his own, truly he is a great leader.

♞ Judge a person's ability from his work

Mullah Nasruddin was 80 years old. He was walking along with a friend. He told his friend, "I am as strong as when I was 20 years old." His friend laughed as said, "Don't bluff. How is it possible?" Mullah replied, "I will prove it to you." He pointed at a huge rock around and said, "You see that rock? When I was 20 years old, I could not lift the rock. Today, at 80 also I cannot lift the rock. So I am as strong as I was before."

Every person is different, so using a common parameter to judge a person's ability may not be accurate or fair. A person's ability is judged by his capacity to do the work assigned to him. "*From the capacity for doing work is the ability of the person judged. And in accordance with the ability, by suitably distributing rank among ministers and assigning place, time and work to them he should appoint all the ministers*," says the *Arthashastra*. So as leaders, before assigning a subordinate a project, take some time to assess the strengths and weaknesses of the person. Delegate the right work to the right person, only then will you get the required results.

Do not get carried away by what you see

All that glitters is not gold. Our mind can fool us. There is a big difference between perception and reality. Therefore, be careful of what you see. Don't believe in what is presented to you. Always start enquiring about reality; the reality would be sometimes the opposite of what is in front of your eyes. It is therefore important to develop the quality of enquiry or *aanvikshiki*. This way you will never be fooled by others.

Chanakya never trusted anyone blindly. Before placing his trust on anyone, he would always think along all dimensions. Additionally, he used spies to verify all the information he had gathered. Society is filled with different kinds of people. And to understand these people only by what they wear, how they speak, how they behave with you necessarily doesn't give you a full picture of who they are. Think beyond what you see.

OUR MIND CAN FOOL US. THERE IS A BIG DIFFERENCE BETWEEN PERCEPTION AND REALITY. THEREFORE, BE CAREFUL OF WHAT YOU SEE. DON'T BELIEVE IN WHAT IS PRESENTED TO YOU.

Inspiration is contagious

Leadership is contagious. A leader can create more leaders. This spirit of leadership starts with an inspiration. When one is inspired, nothing can stop him. That person's life acquires a purpose. They even go on to build great institutions. Such inspired people are proactive. They take quick decisions and enable others also to be fearless and make choices that will benefit everyone.

Chanakya was inspired by a vision, a vision to build a great nation. His inspiration was contagious and he motivated everyone around him, be it his students or his friends. His inspiration was like a fire that spread across the length and breadth of India. This quality to inspire others is called *utsahvardhak*. *Utsah* means inspiration and *vardhak* means to increase. Instead of demotivating someone, we need to inspire people. This is one of the qualities of a great leader.

♞ While wielding power, remember your responsibilities

Many people who get carried away by power do not really understand what power stands for. They get carried away by the glamour of power. A lead position automatically brings certain benefits along with it. Everyone wants to be powerful, but after they get the power, they do not know how to handle it and get fully confused. A powerful leader also has to remember the responsibilities that come along with his position. When one is responsible, his power is put to good use for others, otherwise, it is misused.

THE KING SHOULD ENJOY SENSUAL PLEASURES WITHOUT CONTRAVENING HIS SPIRITUAL GOOD AND MATERIAL WELLBEING.

Chanakya knew the responsibilities of a leader and he wanted a responsible leader for India. Of course, he wanted the king to enjoy his life and not become a workaholic. "*He should enjoy sensual pleasures without contravening his spiritual good and material wellbeing,*" says the *Arthashatra*. If not, one will burn out and will lead an unbalanced life. But getting carried away in merrymaking alone is also not suitable. Therefore, work hard and enjoy the fruits of your labour, too.

♞ Everyone may not have all the qualities

God has a way of getting things done. He gives everyone something unique, which no other person possesses. Your quality is tailor-made only for you. No one in the world is exactly like you. Therefore, focus on that uniqueness. Everyone may not have all the qualities, but everyone has that one quality that can be developed and help us make our life a successful one.

Chanakya knew that one of the essential traits of a leader is the ability to identify the hidden talent of a person. Once the leader understands that, then getting work done by others becomes very easy. Therefore, while selecting a king or even the ministers, Chanakya goes for a full scrutiny of the person, so that the person can be given the right training as per the job requirement. This finally leads to success and happiness of the person and the organization where he works.

♞ Everyone has some qualities. Identify it

If we have understood that everyone has some qualities, the work of a leader is to understand it. How does one do that? There is a method to it — by carefully observing people and how they work. One is to create interest in the work and the other is to identify people interested in the work. Either ways, once the interest is generated, work goes on smoothly. The quality of the work and the personality type of the worker should decide the work to be given to that person.

Chanakya has clearly defined the qualities that are required for each job in Book 2 of the *Arthashastra*. When there is a vacancy, look out for candidates with the required qualifications. On the other hand, one can also look at an employee and create a job opportunity befitting the person. If you are in a position to take decisions, you can do that easily. Most successful organizations or countries create opportunities where people get a chance to develop their qualities.

♞ Everyone cannot be equal

The concept of equality is treating everyone as equal with dignity and honour. However, there is a larger concept of uniqueness over equality. Even identical twins are not equal. They may have many similarities, but each of them will also have some exclusive quality the other does not have. Therefore, instead of seeing equality, start seeing the individuality — therein lays the strength of every person.

Chanakya wrote at length about what can be done to bring out the best in every individual in the *Arthashastra*. He knew that in a society there are various types of people and they have many similarities as well. However, when we start looking for unique qualities in a person, we are acknowledging their personalities. A good leader knows that when you look at people as individuals, you find rare gems.

♞ Do a background check before your recruit people

There is almost always a big difference between what a person says he is and what a person actually is. So, if you are to recruit someone new to your team, check their background first. Candidates usually come with their biodata or CV, making it easy for the recruiter to assess their qualifications. But an intelligent person would go a step forward. Try to crosscheck the CV with their references. With these reference checks, one can also learn a lot more about the candidate that is not on the CV. This way, you will be able to decide whether the said candidate is perfect for the job or not.

In the *Arthashastra*, Book 1, Chapter 12, Rules for Secret Servants and Spies, Chanakya suggests a complete examination of a new employee, before and after he is recruited. So for a leader, knowing the background of a person helps to decide what work he will be suited for and also in what capacity.

♞ Do not make anyone indispensable, including yourself

When you build an organization, it is important to make sure that the organization is not dependent on anyone, including the leader himself, because if the leader leaves one day, the business may collapse. An organization can become a one-man army if it is overly dependant upon its leader. This is not good. Therefore, if you are a leader, make sure do not make any one person fully in-charge of everything. That way, if someone makes a sudden exit, there will be someone else to take over. The work should never suffer on account of a single person. It should go on.

Chanakya spoke about succession planning in the *Arthashastra*. There will always be better leaders who will be available to take your spot when you leave it. So make sure you create those leaders under your leadership. Even in the case of the *amatyas*, the leader makes sure that the work is decentralized and if required it can be given to someone else. *"In case the employee misses the time (of completion) or does the work in a wrong manner, he may complete the work through another,"* says Chanakya. The game is bigger than the player. Similarly, the kingdom is bigger than the king himself.

♘ Identify your next leader before it is too late

Succession planning is not done at the end of the journey. It is done during the journey. If possible, one should start thinking of succession planning even at the beginning of his journey itself. As you are taking up a leadership position, along with many responsibilities, one of the key priorities is to identify the next leader who will replace you when you give up the position. This has to be done much before the time comes for your exit.

The *Arthashastra* suggests the king to identify his heir at the very beginning itself. This awareness has to be brought out during the leadership orientation and training itself. This way, even before one becomes a leader, he starts thinking about the next leader and is mentally prepared for an exit, too, unlike many leaders who never want to retire and not give way to the next generation.

AS YOU ARE TAKING UP A LEADERSHIP POSITION, ONE OF THE KEY PRIORITIES IS TO IDENTIFY THE NEXT LEADER WHO WILL REPLACE YOU WHEN YOU GIVE UP THE POSITION.

♞ After you create, let go

When you create something, naturally you get attached to it. A mother is always attached to her child, no matter how old he grows. An artist is always in love with his painting. An author will always believe that his work is the best in his genre. In the similar manner, leaders are always in love with the organizations they build. After all, which parent is not attached to his children? But, remember, when the child grows up, it is important to let go and let him make his own destiny. As leaders, we should also learn to let go of what we have created.

However, do not handover something you have formed to anybody and everybody. It is also important to find the right person to trust your work with. The next leader should be better than you. That is why it is important to identify the next set of leaders before you leave your office. Once you have decided to let go, you will notice that it is very difficult initially. But slowly, with time, one gets used to it. If you have made the right arrangements for the future, then the organization will continue to grow even after you are gone.

♘ Something small has the potential to become big, big can also become small

Never consider anyone small. Because somebody you consider insignificant today could become someone of significance tomorrow. A seed looks tiny. But if it is planted in the right environment and gets good nourishment, then that same seed can become a massive tree. Therefore, treat people with respect, no matter who they are. In a similar manner, someone who is important does not know how to manage things, can also become a nobody in no time. We all have heard of rags to riches stories, but there are riches to rags stories, too.

Chanakya picked an ordinary boy, Chandragupta, and trained him so well that he not only defeated the arrogant king Dhanananda of Magadha but marched on to became the emperor of united India, founding the Maurya dynasty. And Dhanananda? He lost everything and had to retire to the forest.

♞ Take stock regularly

One of the key qualities of a leader is to take regular stock of everything happening around. We are not only talking about reviewing of accounts and finance but also workers and other inventory. For example, there is a regular audit of finance and accounts in all organizations. However, there are also other audits like performance reviews, cataloguing of physical assets, etc. Checking everything regularly, including the happiness of the people you work with, is the most important role of a leader.

"He (leader) should constantly hold an inspection of their works, men being inconstant in their minds," says Chanakya. If leaders do not supervise things, they will be taken for granted. A dynamic organization is the one where its leader is always active. He will ask the right questions to keep things moving forward. Also, if required, a course correction will be made from time to time. Another way to evaluate the working of your company is to go for surprise checks. A walk around your "kingdom" from time to time is necessary.

♞ Give utmost importance to finance and accounts

When it comes to money matters, Chanakya was quite vigilant. He knew that if the king is lenient and casual about money, then in the long term, it can spell disaster for the kingdom. If finance is not handled properly, there

CHANAKYA GAVE UTMOST IMPORTANCE TO FINANCE AND ACCOUNTS. IN THE DAILY TIMETABLE OF A KING IN THE ARTHASHASTRA, THE FIRST ACTIVITY IN HIS COURT IS TO APPRAISE THE TREASURY.

will be no dearth of problems. Therefore, Chanakya gave utmost importance to finance and accounts. In the daily timetable of a king in the *Arthashastra*, the first activity in his court is to appraise the treasury.

The best part of bookkeeping is that it is it is not just about numbers. Finance statements speak volumes. If one knows how to read a balance sheet, there are many things one will be able to gauge. Looking at the expenses, you will be able to track the outflow of money. If you look at the income side, you will come to know where the wealth is getting created. Control your finances and you have won half the battle of life.

🐎 Understand the difference between finance and accounts

Many people mix up the two words — finance and accounts. While finance is a larger picture of what happens with your money, accounts is the record of the payments you have made. There are many successful businessmen who are not that educated or have the understating of accounting laws and requirements, but they still make a lot of money. That is because they have the financial acumen to understand how money flows and how to get the maximum out of an opportunity.

Chanakya wanted his leaders to learn both finance and accounting and he made sure that daily accounts were maintained in the kingdom. *"He (leader) should check the accounts for each day, group of five days (a week), fortnight, month, four months (quarterly) and a year,"* says *the Arthashastra.* At the same time, this activity helps the leader to develop his understanding about finance. In a kingdom, the *kosha* (treasury) has to be taken good care of. This means that not just bookkeeping, but the understanding of how to fill up the treasury in good and bad times is equally important for a king.

♞ Families form a nation

In India, family is the centre of the society. We take most of our decisions either with the consent of our family or at least we keep them informed about our decisions. Be it marriage, career, or any other special events in our lives, we Indians like to make our folks a part of it. And families put together form a nation.

Chanakya knew this psychology. He was sharp enough to understand that if you want to get things done, you need to involve the family members. Even for nation building, he used family as strategic alliance. Once, a young boy wanted to join Chanakay's new army to defeat Alexander the Great. Chanakya made sure that the boy had his family's permission, especially his mother's, so that he also had the blessings of his family members and is encouraged to fight the war for the nation.

♞ A monk is not just another beggar

On the streets you will find all kinds of people asking for alms. Of these, there are also sanyasis or monks. However, do not treat a monk like any other beggar. Yes, there are many beggars who don the robes of the monks to make money. But a real monk is begging for a bigger reason. For him, it is a privilege to go out and ask for *bhiksha* (alms). Even great men like Swami Vivekananda took *bhiksha* from others.

Chanakya was a teacher and knew the importance of monks in the society. Especially in India, we have given them a very high status. These true monks are serving the society by spreading knowledge to others. Therefore, Chanakya always allowed them special privileges in his kingdom. He allocated them free land to carry out religious activities, teaching and other spiritual chores.

♞ Serve the needy and the spiritual

There are two types of people we need to serve — the needy and the spiritual. Why serve the needy? Because they are dependent on the society for their survival. Educate the poor, provide them employment and other means of social support. So, serving them should be considered as a social responsibility. Similarly, spiritually evolved souls also have to be catered to and by doing so, we have the opportunity to grow spiritually and become wiser.

The *Arthashastra* makes sure that these categories of the needy and the spiritual ones are taken care of with utmost respect. In the Maurya Empire, while the needy were given support to sustain their lives, the spiritual and the wise were invited to the kingdom and given the necessary requirements to carry on with their spiritual activities. Some of them also became mentors and guides to the kings. The concept of *vriddhasanyogah* or being in touch with the knowledgeable ones comes from here (Book 1, Chapter 5, Association with Elders).

Invest in the next generation and their ideas

The next generation will always be different from the current one. This is true for every generation. The new kids on the block bubble with ideas and innovative approaches. However, we take them for granted. At times, we even limit them to our way of thinking. But that is not how it should be. This way, we are limiting ourselves and diminishing the chances of having new ideas to explore. It is important to invest in the next generation and their ideas, because the future belongs to them. Our job is to help them build it.

Chanakya was a great teacher. As a teacher, it is a privilege to work with the next generation. A good teacher learns from the students and helps in shaping the thoughts of the students as well. This is where the real collaboration takes place. The wisdom of the teacher and the new ideas of the students together create a better future for all.

♞ Listen to the wise

The Elderly people are generally discarded and considered useless in today's society. However, they have one advantage over the young generation — experience. The reality is that old people are the asset of any generation. We really do not know how to make the best use of them. The best thing to do is to spend quality time with them. They can give you wisdom and insights gathered from their vast experience. Any amount of time spent with them is not enough.

Chanakya wanted Chandragupta to spend time with the elders. In the company of the aged and the wise, *vriddhasanyogah*, one gets elevated to a different level of thinking. But it is not easy. It takes time and therefore Chanakya advises spending time with the wise to everyone who wants to be a successful leader.

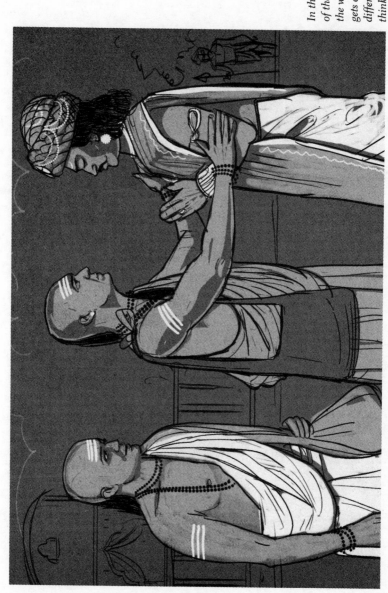

In the company of the aged and the wise, one gets elevated to a different level of thinking.

♞ Live in nature

Nature is beautiful. Nature is for everyone. The best part of nature is that it accommodates everyone. Therefore, in many cultures, it is referred to as 'mother nature'. But the sad part is that we do not take time out to explore it. Especially if one is born in a city, it is difficult to appreciate the value of the role nature plays in one's life. To understand its impact, from time to time live out in the wild. You will come alive all over again.

THE BEST PART OF NATURE IS THAT IT ACCOMMODATES EVERYONE. TO UNDERSTAND ITS IMPACT, FROM TIME TO TIME LIVE OUT IN THE WILD. YOU WILL COME ALIVE ALL OVER AGAIN.

Chanakya had a deep understanding of the power of environment. He was an Ayurveda expert, too. Having spent a lot of time outdoors, he understood its working. He made use of nature and her ploys even in his war strategies. Refer to Book 6, Chapter 6 of the *Arthashatra* where Chanakya talks about the use of a staff, snakes, circle, etc., to counter the enemy. When we know how nature operates, we will know how human beings operate. After all, human beings are a part of nature. And it works vice versa, too.

♞ Respect the intelligent

Intelligent people rule the world. Whether it is countries or organizations, if you look at the *crème de la crème*, you will spot these gifted people. These are the people who actually direct how the future will be for those in that era. Every era is defined by the leaders of that era. And the leader is defined by the kind of bright people who guide them. Therefore, respect the intelligent and know how to use their brainpower and success is guaranteed.

In his books, Chanakya mentions again and again the brilliant gurus who lived before him. Using their experience and wisdom as guiding light, he moves forward in his field of knowledge. From time to time, he quotes these intelligent people in his works. Therefore, if you ask how Chanakya was so intelligent, the answer is that he used the knowledge of the other gifted people around him and built on it.

♞ No one retires, they just change their roles

The concept of retirement is a leftover from the industrial era. If you worked in a factory, there was an age limit after which one has to retire, because working in a factory requires physical agility, which diminishes with age. Today we are living in the knowledge era. Most work is done by the computers anyway. There is no real retirement at all. Yes, of course, one will age and the body will become weak, but today there are many options for the elderly to work without exerting much physical strain on their body. Today's work requirement is more intellectual than physical. One can always continue to work in the capacity of a guide and

Thinking leads to creativity. All inventions and creations have taken their shape first in the mind of the creator.

mentor to others as long as one wishes to. There is no need to retire in this digital age, just change the role to something more comfortable.

The *Arthashastra*, Book 2, Chapter 2 talks about courtesans. With age, courtesans would lose their beauty. But Chanakya did not remove them from their jobs. Instead, he entrusted them with the duty of training the new ones and mentoring them. These senior courtesans were treated with dignity and respect.

♞ Death is inevitable, prepare for it

Once you are born, the only thing certain is your death. Birth is a passport to death. So, if you are aware that one day we all will die, then instead of avoiding it or running scared from it, accept the same with grace and dignity. If you are prepared for the inevitable (mentally and strategically preparing for your death, by taking care of your will, succession planning, etc.), then you will be happy to embrace your old age. Plus, make sure you have prepared yourself spiritually too. Only the body dies, the soul lives on. And so the body should be given up gracefully at the moment of death, with the help of spiritual bliss within you.

Chanakya did something unforgettable before he died. He wrote the *Arthashastra*, which remains till date a masterpiece of all time. So, did Chanakya really die? He made sure that even after his death, he lived through his books. That is the greatness of great men. Death cannot conquer them. In fact, they conquer death through their body of work that is immortal.

♞ Spirituality is not just for the old

There is a myth that spirituality is only for old people, that it is something that you embark on only towards the fag end of your life. In reality, it is the other way around. Spirituality is for the young, so that they know how to lead their life successfully. Spirituality is like a road map. One should refer to it before one starts the journey. What is the use of referring to the road map after the journey is over? Therefore, the younger you are the better it is for you to start the spiritual journey. Better not be too late.

WHAT IS THE USE OF REFERRING TO THE ROAD MAP AFTER THE JOURNEY IS OVER? THEREFORE, THE YOUNGER YOU ARE THE BETTER IT IS FOR YOU TO START THE SPIRITUAL JOURNEY.

Chanakya was nothing less of a spiritual guru. Even though he was an expert in the field of political science, he was truly a person of the spiritual world. And he wanted others also to understand the benefits of spirituality. In the *Arthashastra*, Book 15, Chapter 1, Verse 71, Chanakya says that anyone who practices spirituality in the right spirit will attain this world and the other world too. So never forget that your aim in life should be spiritual success as well.

♞ Being spiritual is not being weak

A myth of spirituality is that spiritual people are weak. This is not true. In fact, spirituality makes you very strong internally. And this internal and mental strength is much more important than the outer physical strength. Great men of achievement were spiritual giants in their own way. Mahatma Gandhi was deeply spiritual. Lokmanya Tilak was another great freedom fighter with inner spiritual energy. So, to succeed in life, become stronger from within first.

The concept of mentioned in the *Arthashastra*, Book 1, Chapter 6, Control Over the Senses, is nothing but making oneself spiritually stronger. However, is not easy to achieve. It takes a lot of mental and physical stamina to become strong spiritually. It is a *tapasya* or a penance that may take ages to accomplish. Chanakya was an evolved spiritual soul and it was only due to this he could accomplish all that we see today as miracles achieved by one person in one lifetime.

♞ Before you destroy, create

It is easy to destroy and very difficult to create anything. But what if we have to destroy something which was worn out and old? In that case, we need to create a backup first before we destroy the old and the useless. For instance, if you have an instrument that is not working properly, do not just discard it. Purchase a new instrument and then the other can be thrown away. If not, you will be left without a choice.

Chanakya knew that Dhanananda had lost his pull as a leader and the kingdom longed for a new leader. Chanakya could have easily killed or dethroned Dhanananda, but he did not do that. He waited patiently for training a new king — Chandragupta. Only then did he think of removing Dhanananda. If a kingdom is without a king, it can lead to more problems. Even if the current leader is bad, create a new one and then replace the old with the new.

🐎 Matured intellect is a virtue

There are many types of intelligences — some have good memory, some are very rational in their approach and some others can come up with multiple solutions for a single problem. But there is one more type of intellect — the one that is mature. Matured intellect is a virtue. What does matured intellect mean? Intellect that is wise and pure, devoid of any selfishness. It is highly spiritual in nature as well. A person with this quality can absorb anything and bring out the best in others for others to benefit from.

The intellect of Chanakya was also highly evolved. He could diagnose any situation from various dimensions, from multiple angles — worldly and spiritual. He also wanted others to develop this matured intellect. Therefore, he taught them *aanvikshiki* — the art of critical thinking. Having developed such a brilliant mind, success always surrounds you.

♞ Clear your doubts, do not keep them

Doubt is a state of mind where it is confused and does not have clarity. To have doubt is natural. But if doubts are not cleared promptly it not only creates confusion but in the long term becomes a handicap. It makes us indecisive. It can also lead to low self-esteem. Therefore, whenever in doubt, clear them. Do not keep your doubts growing. It is better to solve it at the earliest rather than prolonging it.

Chanakya was an advocate of thinking clearly and strategically. *"Coming to know what is known, definite strengthening of what has become known, removal of doubt in case of two possible alternatives, finding out the rest in a matter that is partly known – this can be achieved by external sources,"* he says in the *Arthashastra*. The best way to remove doubt is by using external sources, with outside help. If you cannot solve the problem yourself, talk to someone — a friend, an expert or a trusted partner. Discussing your doubts with someone trustworthy can give you clarity.

♞ How to deal with a crooked competitor

Chanakya is well-known for his 'an eye for an eye and a tooth for a tooth' approach. This means that if a person is being honest with you, you should also be honest with him. But, if he is being dishonest, there is no point in you playing fair. You should tackle the opponent the same way he deals with you. This does not mean that while dealing with a crooked person, you too should become crooked. The idea is to judge the adversary properly before dueling with him.

The whole of the *Arthashastra* talks about the various methods used for defeating enemies. If one strategy does not work, try the next one. At the same time, the same strategy may not work with different people. The wisdom required to tackle the foe is given in the *Arthashastra*. First study the opponent and the patterns in his behaviour. Once you understand the patterns, developing a strategy to overthrow him is easy.

♞ Keep secrets and reveal it at the right time

The beauty of secrets is in safeguarding them. When a secret is out, it loses its value. It is like showing a magic trick to children. They will be impressed as long as you do not reveal the trick behind it. The moment you show them the process behind the magic act, its value is gone. In a similar way, leaders should know how to keep secrets. You will be valued only if you know how to keep a lid on it. However, as a leader, you must also be aware of when to reveal a secret and to whom, to leverage the situation.

In Book 3, Chapter 1, Verse 11 of the *Arthashastra*, Chanakya says, *"In case of secret association, those concluded in secret shall succeed."* For example, take the case of secret service agents. They do a lot of undercover operations to keep a country secure from its enemies. For the smooth running of a country and its safety, it is better that these operations are known only to a few people, revealed only at the right time.

♞ Not punishing those deserving to be punished is being unjust

Criminals in a society deserve to be punished. And if they are not brought under law, it sends a wrong signal to others that the leaders themselves support criminal activities. This makes the leaders look unjust in front of the public. One should therefore know whom to punish, when to punish and what quantum of punishment should be given to the offender. Use the help of law books to know what is just and what is unjust.

In the *Arthashastra*, Chanakya says a good leader should not do various things. One of them is 'reasons for dissatisfaction of subjects by not punishing those deserving to be punished.' When criminals are left to go free or unpunished, there is a sense of insecurity among the common people. The message they get is that anyone can get away with crime and this can lead to disorder in the society or an organization. So, good leaders should penalize the offenders of law, that too, in time.

♞ If you do not know how to judge, seek advice

Leadership is about good judgement. In any given situation, one needs to know how to judge situations and other people. And this becomes even more crucial if you are in a position to take decisions. So, when you are alerted to a problem and you are not able to arrive at the right judgement, what do you do? Just seek advice from the right people.

Chanakya has given the framework within which the judge should make decisions in the Book 3 of the *Arthashastra*. A judge should not be considered a super human being. He can also make mistakes. So a well-informed and wise judge is required at every stage. However, he can seek advice from previous judges and experts (*vriddhasanyogah*). He can also consult the various law books available to him.

♞ Listen to children

Children have the ability to think differently since they do not carry the burden of having past experiences like their elders. For the same reason, their ideas can also be original. That is why children are always innovative and creative. In their innocence there is an openness to adapt to change very fast. They can also show you some simple aspects of an issue that you may have overlooked. There is a saying, "Don't be childish, be child-like", meaning be mature, but retain your originality from your childhood.

"A wise man should make use of the sensible words of even the child," says Chanakya. Listen to children more carefully than you listen to older people, because even though elders have more experience, they are clouded by their past. Sometimes the past is not enough to build the future. For building the future, one needs to have a new approach, which sometimes children can provide.

♞ If you cannot ask directly, ask indirectly

Many people get frustrated in life because they cannot get what they want. But in reality, what they want can be easily achieved. Most of the time, they cannot get what they want only because they are too shy to ask. Your goal is just one step away. Therefore, if you cannot ask for what you want directly, ask indirectly. This is a strategy that will help you achieve your goals. If you cannot ask verbally, ask it in writing. It is much easy to communicate in writing. If you cannot ask yourself, make the request through a friend who can get the work done for you.

MOST OF THE TIME, PEOPLE CANNOT GET WHAT THEY WANT ONLY BECAUSE THEY ARE TOO SHY TO ASK. IF YOU CANNOT ASK YOURSELF, MAKE THE REQUEST THROUGH A FRIEND.

Chanakya was a master communicator and he would always get his work done either directly or indirectly. When Chanakya was seeking help for his battle against Alexander the Great, he realized that most kings did not want to help him. This was because most of them did not understand his vision. Therefore, he made his request in an indirect way. He approached the ministers of those kings and they in turn managed the approval from their respective kings. This way, he got the support he wanted to defeat Alexander's army.

♞ Understand the mass psychology

There are a few rare qualities that leaders should have. One of them is the understanding of 'mass psychology'. People in groups think in a certain way. If one is able to get an insight into how human beings in a group think and react, success can be easily achieved. Politicians play on this mass psychology to get votes and win elections. Sometimes they even confuse people to achieve their goals.

Chanakya used these techniques of mass psychology to defeat his enemies as well. When he wanted to take over the kingdom of the enemy, he used the weapon of diplomacy. He would often confuse people in order to achieve his objectives. It is called 'management by confusion'. His idea was to confuse the opponent in such a way he has no idea what to do next and in the meantime, get what you want and get out.

♞ Have multiple advisors but not too many

One cannot move ahead in life alone. We all require friends and advisors along our journey. They are essential to ease our pains and show us some beautiful scenery along the way as we travel. The more friends you have in life, the better it is, so that you can share the joys and burdens of the journey with the others. But remember to choose your friends carefully. Be friendly with everyone, but your true friends should be a few only.

Chanakya knew that having advisors for a king is very important. They play a critical role in the success of the leader. He also warns that the leader should not have just one guide, but multiple, to have a more rounded perspective of any situation. However, too many opinions to choose from can also be confusing. *"Holding a consultation with only one, he may not be able to reach a decision in difficult matters. With more counsellors, it is difficult to reach decisions and maintain secrecy,"* says the *Arthashastra* on the topic of counsellors.

🐎 Continuous improvement guarantees progress

One cannot sit back and say, "I have achieved success." That is the most dangerous situation to be in. That kind of attitude can hamper your progress and halt your journey midway. Even if you have achieved success and are at the peak, remember to keep walking. Because, there are many more peaks to climb. If there are no more challenges, you should create new ones. Life is an ongoing journey and one should have goals, no matter how big or small, throughout the way to have a meaningful life. Therefore, one needs to focus on continuous improvement. This guarantees progress. Be your own benchmark for success.

Chanakya wanted his king to be not just a winner but a continuous winner. It is not just a hypothetical statement, but something that can be achieved in the real world. There were kings whom Chanakya called 'vijigishu' — world conqueror. To achieve something of great magnitude, one has to do things in a way the others have never done. One needs to find territories that have never existed before and play games that others have never played.

♞ Be excellent in your words and deeds

Leadership is not just lip service. It is about action. If you have promised someone something, it has to be delivered. Therefore, when someone reaches a leadership position, the words and deeds of the person counts. So be true to every word that you say, and make sure your deeds are in line with those words. Keep your word, fulfil your promises, even at the cost of your life.

According to Chanakya, one of the leadership qualities is the ability to keep promises. However, one needs to think hundred times before making a promise. It is better not to make a promise that you cannot deliver than to make one and break it. And whatever you do, do it well. A leader is always in search of excellence. Excellence becomes a way of life. When Chanakya created the India of his dreams, it was so well done that we remember it even today.

♞ A king protects his kingdom

The king is the overall protector of his kingdom. He is responsible for the welfare and security of his people. Chanakya gives us strategies as to how to protect the people and a kingdom together. The *Arthashastra* says, "A king protects the kingdom only when he himself is protected from persons near him and his enemies." So, in order to protect the kingdom, first of all he has to protect himself from the dangers lurking nearby.

A leader has two types of rivals — internal and external. Look at the stories of assassinations of various leaders. Most of the time, it is carried out by an insider or someone close to the leader. Because of it, a leader has to always be vigilant and alert. The next is the threat from the competitors outside who wants to take over the organization/kingdom. One needs to have plans to defeat both internal and external enemies.

♞ Educating the child is the duty of his parents

Like animals and birds, human beings also care for their children. But there is a difference between the animal kingdom and human civilization — the way they train the offspring. Animals train their children to hunt for food and sustain themselves, while human beings have to teach their children much more than about just eating, drinking and protecting themselves from enemies. They have to train them in moral standards; they have to groom their children to become cultured inviduals.

Educating and training a child is the duty of its parents. The first lessons of a child start at home. The next level of training is given at schools, where expert teachers will educate him on various subjects. But good parents also give their children training in ethical thinking (*aanvikshiki*). One has to instill moral and ethical codes of conduct in his children and make sure all their activities are legal. Chanakya shaped an education system where this was the foundation of good parenting and schooling.

🐎 Teach your children how to be spiritually and materially successful

It is a misconception that one has to only teach their children how to be successful materially. It is also equally important to teach them to be spiritually successful. Therefore, a good parent or teacher will teach the young ones both. Note that spiritual success should come before material success, because a child with a strong spiritual foundation will be able to handle material success without it getting to his head.

A successful person should not have ego. Chanakya wanted his future leaders to be ego-free. During the training of the princes, disciplining them is very essential. *"For, like* the piece of wood eaten by worms, the royal family, with its princes undisciplined, would break the moment it is attacked," says the Arthashastra. Without discipline, a person will not become internally strong. An internally strong person can withstand any type of attack — physical or psychological.

♞ Youth is power, youth is energy. Give it direction

A high-powered engine is useless if it does not know which direction it has to go. So is the case with the youth of any nation. The younger generation has the benefit of age with them and is full of energy. However, without direction, energy is useless. So, in order to give them direction, work with them and mentor them. Swami Chinmayananda used to say, "Youth is not useless, it is used less. Youth is not careless, it is cared [for] less."

Chanakya knew the power of the youth. When various kings, along with Dhanananda, did not support him, his only hope was the youth of the country. He moulded them, gave them direction and strategy and finally defeated Alexander the Great, who was on his way to conquer the

THE YOUNGER GENERATION HAS THE BENEFIT OF AGE AND IS FULL OF ENERGY. HOWEVER, WITHOUT DIRECTION, ENERGY IS USELESS. TO GIVE THEM DIRECTION, WORK WITH THEM AND MENTOR THEM.

world. In the same way, every generation requires guidance.
Once they get a direction, they can create wonders.

♞ Educate the youth with the dangers of vices

Children are very innocent. But this innocence and curiosity
may lead them to danger if they are not cautioned. Once
you educate them about the dangers around them or the
consequences of their actions, they get scared and stay away
from the people and events that frighten them.

The youth is generally attracted to new things and ideas.
There is also a danger of them walking off in the wrong
direction. If not corrected in time, vices will impact the
overall personality of the person and corrupt him. Plus,
the impact would stay for life. And immoralities can ruin
a whole generation. So, Chanakya would keep an eye on
the youngsters of his kingdom. With the use of negative
images and stories, he used to distract the youth from
the pitfalls surrounding them. Always educate the young
about bad habits and show them the right way to grow into
responsible adults.

♞ Train the youth to be leaders

There is a misconception that if you do not have enough
experience, you cannot be a leader. This statement has been

proven wrong time and again across the globe where young leaders have emerged and made history, be it in politics, business or in the field of science. The younger the better is the formula many apply today. The youth has inherent leadership qualities, it only needs to be nurtured. Therefore, train the youth to be leaders.

Chanakya did exactly that — be it Chandragupta Maurya or his other students, he trained all of them to become great leaders. He had faith in them and through careful training modules, he created his own leadership development programs. His training method is detailed in the *Arthashastra*. If you commit to training the next generation to become future leaders, they will turn out to be much better leaders than you are, and the world will benefit from it.

♞ Teach the youth to take decisions. Let them learn through their mistakes

In the Indian army, there is a golden rule: make mistakes, but make sure you take decisions. Your decisions need not be right every time, but it is important to call your shots. Decisions do come with a risk of failure. However, without experience, there is no growth. Good or bad, own your decisions and learn from your mistakes. Avoiding making up your mind about something you have to do is the worst you can do to yourself. If you make the right call, you will achieve success, and if something goes wrong, you will learn from your mistake, furthering your wisdom.

Chanakya wanted his disciples to take their own decisions. He allowed them room for mistakes as those are inevitable during the process. However, he used to keep an eye on their activities. He would carefully mentor and guide them towards success. *"He should hear (at once) every urgent matter, (and) not put it off. An (affair) postponed becomes difficult to settle or even impossible to settle,"* urges Chanakya in the *Arthashastra*. Do not postpone your decisions. Make up your mind. It will only get difficult later on.

🐎 Keep an eye on your children

Children are full of energy. They cannot sit in one place for long. They need some activity or the other on a continuous basis. If you are a parent, you will understand that one needs to keep an eye on kids at all times or otherwise it can prove to be dangerous. They can get into accidents or something unfortunate may happen to them. Therefore, the real challenge of parenting is to watch over your children, yet train them to become independent.

ONE NEEDS TO KEEP AN EYE ON KIDS AT ALL TIMES. THE REAL CHALLENGE OF PARENTING IS TO WATCH OVER YOUR CHILDREN, YET TRAIN THEM TO BECOME INDEPENDENT.

Once a king asked Chanakya to come and meet him. He sent back a reply, "Tell your king I cannot come now, I am busy creating future kings." Chanakya was a teacher, and a teacher is like a parent who has to keep an eye on his students. He knew that taking care of the students was more important a job than meeting a king. If we invest in spending time with children, the returns will be very high as they go on to become well-rounded, successful individuals in the future.

When the youth is ready, make them in-charge

Teach the youth to be leaders. Prepare them to lead. When the youth is ready, make them in-charge; give them leadership positions. But the key question is, when do you hand over the full charge to the youth? When do you know they are ready to take up the position of leadership? This is not an easy question to be answered. It all depends on the maturity and readiness of the person. And that has to be judged from person-to-person basis.

On a plane, usually there are at least two pilots — the captain and the co-pilot or the first officer. The captain is usually a senior pilot with more experience and flying time under his belt. The first officer is someone junior to the captain, whose job is to assist the captain. The captain is ultimately responsible for everything that happens on the flight. He also flies the plane for much of the trip. At some point during the flight, when the captain is sure the first officer will be able to manage flying on his own, he hands over the controls to him. The same way, Chanakya made his student Chandragupta Maurya the emperor of India under his guidance.

♞ Work with children as they are the future

When we invest in children, we are investing in the future. As parents, we do many things for our children. We provide them with food, clothing and shelter. We also enroll them in good schools. We do financial planning for their future. However, many of us forget to spend time with them. We think that by doing everything else we become good parents. That is not true. Your time is the best investment for your child's bright future. This cannot be outsourced.

When your children are small, they will demand all of your time and attention. However, once they have grown up, even if you want to spend time with them, they will not want to stay with you. This is the irony of life. So it is better to spend time with them when they are young, be it helping with their studies or any school/college project they undertake. *"He (king) should strive to give training to the prince,"* says Chanakya in the *Arthashastra*. Chanakya advised that in spite of his busy schedule, a king needs to spend time with his children because they are the future of his kingdom.

♞ Do not just hope, create the future

Hope is a good thing to have. In all the negative stages of life, optimism is the only thing that keeps us going. But, only hoping and doing nothing is dangerous. One needs to have hope, but along with that one needs to work hard and create the future that he aspires for. Nothing happens on its own. One needs to plan and carefully put the plan into action. Finally, one needs to achieve the results, too.

Chanakya also had to face adversities in life. Yet he did not lose hope. He sat down and planned an India of the future. He was not just a dreamer but an achiever. He worked day and night. Even when a single soul did not support him, even in times of defeat, he kept his cool. Like Chanakya, leaders cannot afford to lose hope. In fact, leaders are the only hope. When they get up and work, others also feel the motivation to keep going. Hope followed by action is the only way forward.

♞ Keep your head above your heart

We are all emotional by nature. And there is nothing wrong with having emotions. But the danger is in getting carried away by emotions. Have emotions but do not become emotional. Have sentiments but do not become sentimental. God has given us heart, but along with that he has given us a brain. Therefore, use your head while taking decisions. If you are a leader, it is even more crucial to take logical steps ahead, not just emotional.

HAVE EMOTIONS BUT DO NOT BECOME EMOTIONAL. HAVE SENTIMENTS BUT DO NOT BECOME SENTIMENTAL. GOD HAS GIVEN US HEART, BUT ALSO ALONG WITH THAT HE HAS GIVEN US A BRAIN.

Chanakya taught *aanvikshiki* to his students. This is the method of logical thinking. According to *aanvikshiki*, one has to think not just strategically but also by keeping the head clear. He also suggests that *sankya* (numbers) is a part of *aanvikshiki*. So, one has to be driven by facts while making decisions. To have all your facts in front of you while deciding on a matter is essential to make successful decisions.

♞ Check the quality of work completed

People make huge promises. These promises are usually made to get a job or a project. But remember, no one will say bad things about himself. People always put their best self in front of the world. One should not get carried away by the CV of a person. Have you ever seen a CV that lists the failures of a person? Therefore, before offering a job to a candidate, check the competency of the person. And make sure you check the quality after the completion of the job, too.

Chanakya was not to take any person on face value. Even if he appointed someone on a particular post, he kept an eye on him. Before making anyone permanent, he used to try them on a temporary basis. Probably this is how the concept of probation period came up. In the chapter named *Amatya Utpatti* in Book 2 of the *Arthashastra*, Chanakya talks about conducting various tests even for high profile candidates like ministers before he allowed them to get close to the king. Also, after these officials were made permanent, he used to test the quality of their work before he promotes them again.

♞ Sometimes not having a plan is a good plan

It is good to plan. If you fail to plan, you plan to fail. Have a good plan in life. Have a direction and focus. But then, be flexible. Do not become rigid with your plans. Just do not make your plans in such a way that you lose focus on the goal, the big picture, the overall objective. So, sometimes you have to let go of your plan. Therefore, at times, not to have a plan is a good plan. That does not mean you are lazy. Actually, you are allowing God to make a plan for you.

Even when Chanakya made plans, he kept room for flexibility. This flexible attitude is evident in the way he planned the king's daily schedule. In the *Arthashastra*, Book 1, Chapter 19, Rules of the King, while he defines every activity of the king for the day, with the time allocated to each activity, he also keeps it flexible — *"Or, he should divide the day and night and (work) in conformity with his capacity and carry out the tasks."*

♞ You must test the purity of gold and trustworthiness of people

Never trust blindly. There are times when your most trusted friend or colleague cheats you. When Chanakya was guiding Chandragupta Maurya in ruling his kingdom, he had put in various measures to ensure that everything is under control. He even tested the purity of the gold that came into the treasury. Similarly, he trusted people only after testing them.

There are times when we get confused between trust and test. It is important to trust. Without the trust factor, nothing is possible. When we board an aircraft or a train, we trust the driver completely that he will take us safely to the correct destination. If we do not trust the driver, we will not be able to travel in peace.

♞ Set a standard where a standard never existed

Imagine you were made in-charge of a completely new project, a project that was never done before, something that never existed. And you are given full freedom to create the whole thing as you wish. Now, we can look at this scenario in two ways — either as a challenge or as an opportunity. You will be the first person to do something that was never done before. You can set a standard where a standard never existed.

Chanakya was a leadership guru. He believed that all of

Chanakya tested the purity of even the gold that came to the king's treasury.

us can be leaders and can create something that never existed before. He knew that creation is not easy. Yet, once we make something, others will take a look at it and it may even be duplicated. When Chanakya formed a united India, he made it the best. When he shaped kings, they went on to lead the whole world (*Vijigishu*). Thus, take a leaf out of Chanakya's life and think of becoming the best, and become the best for others to follow.

CHANAKYA WAS A LEADERSHIP GURU. HE BELIEVED THAT ALL OF US CAN BE LEADERS AND CAN CREATE SOMETHING THAT NEVER EXISTED BEFORE. HE ALSO KNEW THAT CREATION IS NOT EASY.

♞ Every person's productivity should be measured

The things that are not measured do not progress. Only if you are able to measure will you know if you are successful or not. For instance, if you do not get marks or grades in studies, will you be able to know where you stand? Without scores, everything is very generic. In the same way, every person's productivity should also be measured. In an organization, every person has a job to do. And that work has to be measured. Based on the assessment, you will be able to find whether that person is fit for the job or not.

"*From the capacity for doing work is the ability of the person judged,*" says Chanakya in the *Arthashastra*. When

we measure the work a person has done, we also know
the capacity of the person. Chanakya wanted to know the
capacity of the people he employed. He measured their
performances and then based on that he used to promote
the good performers and allocate them more work and
responsibilities. This way, each and every person in an
organization will have a measured way to success.

♞ Every person must contribute, even if a little

In the *Ramayana*, there is a story of a squirrel. When
Lord Rama's army was trying to build a bridge from
Rameshwaram to Sri Lanka, each person was contributing
his share of the work load. A tiny squirrel was watching the
goings-on and he also wanted to be a part of the activity.
So, he went and dipped himself in the sea, came back
and rolled in the mud, and then went straight back to the
sea again to wash himself and deposit the mud in the sea
water. He was doing his bit to build the bridge. Lord Rama
noticed his efforts. He lifted the squirrel and patted him on
the back for his contribution. According to the lore, that is
how the squirrel got his stripes.

In the process of nation building, too, we need everyone,
does not matter whether someone is big or small. Only
when each person does his duty towards the nation will the
nation grow. Chanakya knew this. A farmer who works on

his land and the soldier who fights at the border are equally important. A mother, a factory worker or a teacher at the school — each of them are nation builders in their own ways. What is your contribution towards nation building? Think...

♞ Everyone has a role to play, everyone should know their role

Role clarity is most important while doing any job. Do your job well. But make sure you know your job before committing to it. Doing someone else's work instead of one's own may create confusion. Also, not doing one's own part will also lead to chaos. In the *Ramayana*, Lord Hanuman was told to go to Lanka and check on Sita. His job was only to go as a messenger and not bring her back. That was Lord Rama's job.

Chanakya knew that every person has a duty (*dharma*). And we should do our duty very well. The role of each person in the society has been clearly defined in the *Arthashastra*. A student should study well. A householder should take care of his family and earn money for the well-being of others. A teacher should teach well. Chanakya has meticulously listed out the duties of each person at every stage of his life. Follow your duty and role in life, and everybody, including you, will be happy.

♞ Promote those with leadership qualities

When you are a leader, one of your priorities should be to identify the next set of leaders. They are always around you. You need to have an eye to notice who are those people in your organization with leadership potential. When you see such qualities of leadership in people, they should be promoted. They should be given some higher responsibilities, a better job profile or a bigger project. Watch them, observe them and see how they are doing. This way, you will automatically nurture the next generation.

Chanakya used to give small responsibilities to his students. In his *gurukul,* he entrusted his older and brighter to students to tutor their juniors, so those older students developed leadership qualities quickly. They later went on to become great teachers and *acharyas* themselves.

♞ Everyone should get an opportunity to prove their leadership qualities

Sometimes we get an opportunity to prove our mettle or sometimes we just have to create those opportunities ourselves. People become frustrated because they believe they are denied opportunities to grow. Sometimes they blame the boss at the workplace or sometimes it is the backstabbing friends or sometimes it is just plain bad luck. But then everyone gets an opportunity to prove our leadership qualities. Just be on the lookout for a sign and when such an opportunity comes, grab it with both hands.

Swami Chinmayananda used to say, "When opportunity knocks at our door, either we are outside or sleeping inside." One should be able to look at such opportunities as a chance to succeed. Chanakya saw an opportunity when he noticed that Dhananand was a bad leader. He knew he could create something that never existed before — good leadership. Chandragupta Maurya was his masterpiece created for other leaders to duplicate.

"WHEN OPPORTUNITY KNOCKS AT OUR DOOR, EITHER WE ARE OUTSIDE OR SLEEPING INSIDE." ONE SHOULD BE ABLE TO LOOK AT SUCH OPPORTUNITIES AS A CHANCE TO SUCCEED.

♞ Create opportunities for others to prove their leadership qualities

One should be large-hearted in order to become a good leader. And good leaders are not insecure. They are forever ready to create more leaders. So, if you are a leader, create opportunities for others to prove their leadership qualities. Thus, you will be a role model to others. When there are many leaders in an organization, it is a good situation to be in. Leaders will bring their own followers and it will help the organization to flourish.

Chanakya says, *"Rulership can be successfully carried out (only) with the help of associates. One wheel alone does not turn."* A leader cannot be a one-man show. He requires associates, people who will help him in his journey. And it is better to have other leaders as associates, so you will have better quality discussions and together each one of you will grow. When you create leaders, you are duplicating your knowledge and experience. You are replicating yourself.

♞ Born leaders also require training

All men are not equal, some are born extraordinary. There are those who are born leaders. However, being a born leader is not enough. Born leaders should be trained and given an opportunity to shine and then only can they become successful. There are many people with leadership potential, but without proper guidance, their talent is lost. And even if they are trained well, without an opportunity to show what they have learned, they are still a failure.

Therefore, the only thing to do with born leaders is to find good mentors. Chanakya was one such leadership coach, mentor and guide. He knew that it is important for people with potential, like Chandragupta, to be groomed. This grooming is both spiritual and psychological. When both these aspects are instilled in the students, they become excellent leaders.

♞ Without training, even the best is useless

Training should be an essential part of any organization. Training is very important even for running a country. Governments have human resources departments too. Their main aim is to train their people in various aspects — be it education, research, skill development or something else. Without training, nobody can progress, even the best will become useless. You may have good leadership potential, but if you do not polish it, it will become useless.

Chanakya was a master trainer. He not only believed in training but in *continuous* training. It is the law of nature that various things get outdated. So, if you want to deal with change, you need training. Right from the top till the bottom everyone needs training. The best is to start from the top itself. So, the best training should be given to the king himself. Therefore, the first book of the *Arthashastra* is called 'Vinayadhikarikam' (The topic of training for the king).

♞ Training imparted has to be of high standards

Training given should be of world class. For most organizations, training given to their staff is never the top priority. If you provide top-notch training to your employees, you will benefit from it in the future. Training is always a long-term plan. The approach cannot be a "quick fix". It

TRAINING IS ALWAYS A LONG-TERM PLAN. THE APPROACH CANNOT BE A "QUICK FIX". IT IS LIKE BRINGING UP A CHILD. IT TAKES LOT OF TIME INITIALLY.

is like bringing up a child. It takes lot of time initially. Yet, when the child grows up to a well-rounded individual, you will know that the effort was worth it.

Chanakya knew that high standards of training also depended on the students who were being trained. In the *Arthashastra*, he says, *"(From) Continuous study ensures a trained intellect, from intellect (comes) practical application, (and) from practical application (results) self- possession."* Training sharpens one's intellect. But that is not enough, one has to apply the intellect. Only then does he become an expert in his field.

♞ Train with the best

There was a person who went to a new city. He had learnt flute and wanted a new teacher in the new city. So, he approached a well-known flautist. When asked about the fees, the master said, "For new students, ₹500 per month. For an old student, ₹5000 per month." Shocked, the person asked, "Did I hear it wrong? I have already learnt to play it, so I should be charged less." The master replied, "You heard it right. It takes ten times the effort to undo what you have already learnt. So, for an old student, the charge is ten times the regular fees."

If you want to learn something, learn it from the best. When you get the best teacher, you will grow much faster than everyone. An expert teacher not only has the required experience, but he also has the insight. This is something of a rare combo. Even if you have all the money in the world, you may not get the best teacher. But, if you are ready to pay anything (even your life), the best teacher will come to you. This is the reason Chanakya only took in the best students, because he was the best teacher.

♞ Train persistently

The objective of education is not to get a good job after completing school or college. The main aim of education should be character building, not income, prestige or power. The best of the lot continue their education even after they are done with their studies. The same way, training in any field has to be forever. Even if you have got the best training already, continue it throughout your life.

In the chapter describing the routine of a king in the *Arthashastra* (Book 1, Chapter 19), Chanakya suggests continuous training. According to the master strategist, the king has to go and inspect his army and troops again and again. This is a part of his training. Chanakya knew that continuous training leads to perfection. Even an expert has to learn and update his knowledge day after day to stay on top of his game.

♞ Practice forever

Some things we have to practice till we die. There is no choice. Even if we are old, we have to continue doing certain things. For instance, brushing the teeth, taking a bath, eating, etc., are things we learn as children, but then continue to do as long as we live. Similarly, our talents and hobbies, be it music, dance or any other art form, if we do not practice it regularly, even the best of us will lose touch over time.

The *Arthashastra* defines *swadharma* as something which is natural to a person and *swadhyaya* as self-study. Both are essential for a person and have to be practiced forever. Never come up with excuses for not following the practice. It is like exercise, it has to be done daily and consistently. And that is why they say that practice makes a person perfect.

♞ Without practice even the best will lose

Once there was a cricket team who were world champions. They went on a series tour to another country. The performance of this world-class team was pathetic during the series and it shocked the fans. They lost the entire series due to poor performance. Their fans back home were disappointed, to say the least. Post the match when they analyzed their performance, they realized that they had not practiced before the series began. They had spent their time partying and going out. After all, they were the world champions, who could defeat them?

This kind of a thought progress is very dangerous. Even if you are the best, do not take it for granted that you will be a winner forever. Just go out and practice again and again. World champions know that getting to the top is the very difficult and it is even more difficult to remain at the top. So practice continuously or even the best will lose the race. Chanakya reminded his students not to forget the important leadership lesson — *abhyas* (practice). It is something that keeps you going, forever and ever.

EVEN IF YOU ARE THE BEST, DO NOT TAKE IT FOR GRANTED THAT YOU WILL BE A WINNER FOREVER. JUST GO OUT AND PRACTICE AGAIN AND AGAIN.

Work should be completed on time

Project delayed is project failed. Projects get delayed because of inadequate planning and wrong execution. A good project manager will look into various factors before starting any project, most importantly, the time frame within which the project has to be completed. Other aspects like finance, man power, etc., are also critical. But at the end of everything, if the project is not completed on time, it cannot be considered a successful project.

"The means of starting undertakings (assignments/ projects), the excellence of men and materials, deciding suitable place and time, provision against failure, accomplishment of the work," says Chanakya in Book 1 of the *Arthashastra*. When

you plan a project, you have to consider every detail. When the details are worked out beforehand, nothing misses your attention. It is the trademark of a good project manager who accomplishes any task on time.

♞ Work not completed by one should be given to another

In any big project, there will be multiple people involved. Big projects are also time-consuming. It is natural that during such humongous projects stretching for years, people may leave and some may join afresh. Therefore, Chanakya says that work not completed by one should be given to another, which means that no project should be totally dependent on any one person. In case somebody leaves midway, work should not suffer.

THE PEOPLE WHO JOIN THE ORGANIZATION SHOULD WORK TOWARDS ACHIEVING THE VISION OF THE ORGANIZATION.

And no person should feel that the work depends on him alone. Make sure that you are ready to exit at any given moment and the work should go on irrespective of you being around or not. Great organizations are built like that. They look at the big picture. They look at something larger beyond the people involved. The vision of the organization should be bigger than anything else. The people who join the organization should work towards achieving that common vision.

♞ Supervise the work of others

Once there was a person who had a very good team in his organization. He used to work closely with his team members and was an ideal leader. One day, he thought that now that his team is good and hardworking, he can sit back and relax. So, he just delegated the work to his subordinates and did not oversee the progress of his team. He noticed after some time that his hardworking team had become unproductive.

"Even the most productive team will become lazy if the leader does not supervise the work of others," Chanakya says about the importance of supervision in Book 2 of the *Arthashastra*. As a leader, you can delegate the work to the best team you have, but if they are not monitored regularly and closely, even the best team will become direction less. Therefore, leaders cannot just relax. They have to be alert, vigilant and guide others at all times.

♞ Quality and quantity are both important

Which is more important, quality or quantity? In reality, both are important. From quantity comes quality. That means only if there are many to choose from will you find quality among those. For instance, if there is a class of 60 students, the best ones, the quality students, will come from that batch of 60. One cannot insist that only quality students should be there in the class. Therefore, it is important to manage both quality and quantity. They are interdependent.

Chanakya had taught many students. And from those emerged the leaders of quality, like Chandragupta Maurya. If he had focused only on one student, he would probaby not have got the best ones like Chandragupta. It is like finding a pearl. One needs to search a lot to shells to get that one pearl, that rare gem, which stands out. It is similar to a scientific experiment; only through trial and error will you find the best and succeed in the process.

🐎 Quantity first

Do not worry too much about quality in the beginning. It will develop in the process. But yes, one has to be quality-conscious from day one. If you obsess about quality, the danger is, you may never start. So hit the road and start driving. No one will become a perfect driver from day one. But slowly and steadily, once you get the hang of how to handle a car, your driving will become smooth. Life is a journey, starting with quality and moving towards quality.

Chanakya was a perfectionist. He wanted everything to be in order. Yet, he also knew that all the people whom he came across may not have the same outlook. However, he had patience, so he worked slowly towards his goal. He wanted the best for his kingdom. He built the nation of his dreams slowly and steadily. At the end, what he built was to last forever.

♞ Judges must have high moral standards

The judicial system of any nation is a very important part of that society. Judges in any society is given a lot of importance and respect because they are the ones responsible for deciding on cases that comes in front of the court of law. In any good system, there has to be a fair trial and then finally the right verdict has to be given. For this to happen, judges should have high moral standards. Therefore, selection and training of the judges was very critical for Chanakya who designed a very good legal system during his time.

In the *Arthashastra*, Book 3 is called 'Dharmasthiya' (topic concerning judges). In the same book, there are various examples on how judges need to make their decisions. Some of the rulings are easy because of the history of such cases in the past while sometimes they can be very difficult decisions if they are happening for the first time. However, in every case, one has to use critical thinking, *aanvikshiki*. Only then good verdicts can be made.

♞ Train the right people

Do not waste your time training the wrong people. You cannot make a dog fly and a fish to climb a tree. That is not natural for them. So train a person in what he has a natural inclination for. A good teacher would carefully study the student and check if he is fit to be trained. Only those who are trainable should be trained. Or it is a misery for both the teacher and the student. It is best to judge the disposition before and then start the training; make sure there is water at the base before starting to dig the well.

There comes a time when a new leader is needed. At that time, it is important to check for those who have the leadership potential. Those people have to be then trained and moulded. Chanakya always selected only the best and trainable children as his students. And he found many, one of them being Chandragupta Maurya. According to Chanakya, *"When he (prince) is ready for it (knowledge), experts should train him."* Give the world's best training to those who deserve it. One should not compromise on the training at all.

Borrow if you must, but payback later

THERE WILL BE TIMES OF SHORTAGE AND CRISIS IN EVERY PERSON'S LIFE. WHEN THOSE EMERGENCIES OCCUR, DO NOT STOP YOUR WORK OR NEGLECT YOUR DUTY BECASUE OF LACK OF FUNDS.

Money is very important for survival. There will be times of shortage and crisis in every person's life. When those emergencies occur, do not stop your work or neglect your duty due to lack of funds. Borrow if you must to handle the situation and make sure to pay it back. For example, if someone in the family suddenly meets with an accident, he needs to be taken to the hospital immediately. It is not the time to worry about money.

Borrowing in such situations is not something to be ashamed of. Decisions like these should not be based on financials. But make sure to pay the lender back.

In a chapter of the *Arthashastra* named Setting Up of Revenue by the Administrator (Book 2, Chapter 6), Chanakya does not condone money borrowed for the right reasons. There are two types of debts — good debt and bad debt. A good debt is the one where money is borrowed for the right reason and also paid back in time as promised. A bad debt is where the borrowed money is misused and also not returned. Borrow for the right reasons and do not get caught in bad debt situations.

❧ Borrowing is better than begging

'Beg, borrow or steal' is a common idiom used to indicate the necessity of something. However, stealing is not right, and borrowing is better than begging. There are a few people in our culture who are allowed to beg —the monks and mendicants. They have no source of income and they beg only for their basic survival. Such sanyasis are also respected and highly honoured. But for other types of people, especially the householders, begging is not dignified. So if required, borrow, but do not beg.

In the *Arthashastra*, Chanakya underlines that a student of the Vedas must keep the vow of living on alms only. On the other hand, the duty of a householder is to earn his living. A student should concentrate on his studies and not engage in work or otherwise his mind will be distracted. An able-bodied householder should work hard and earn for his family and not beg for alms.

♞ Do not commit suicide

Death is not a solution to any problem. Those who run away from problems of life will have to face it in one way or the other at some point. And most people consider suicide as the easiest way to solve any problem. This is a myth. By committing suicide, you are actually creating more problems, especially for your family and other near and dear ones.

It is better to face problems with square shoulders. Why run away from this world? We have to be in this world and come out a winner. Do not accept defeat. The whole world may be against you, but trust in God and you will emerge a winner. Chanakya was against taking one's own life. In fact, he was so angry with those people who committed suicide that he instructed that their bodies should not be cremated as their actions reflected an undignified way of living and dying.

ACKNOWLEDGEMENTS

My special thanks to Jaico Publishing House and the whole team who worked behind this book.

Special thanks to Akash Shah and Ashwin Shah, two wonderful people who inspire me to keep on writing more books on Chanakya.

I would also like to thank…

Sandhya Iyer, my editor. She keeps pushing me to scale new heights in my writing. I write books and she polishes them so that they shine when they come out.

The whole editorial team at Jaico. I know how difficult it is to edit and make Chanakya's wisdom simple and readable.

Vijay Thakur, the head of sales at Jaico, and other various branch heads across India and their sales teams. After all, these people make sure my books sell well and get into the bestseller charts.

And of course, you, my readers, who have faith in me and the wisdom of Chanakya.

My salutations to each one of you.